Living Wisely

Living Wisely

Further advice from Nāgārjuna's *Precious Garland*

Sangharakshita

indhorse Publications

Published by
Windhorse Publications
169 Mill Road
Cambridge
CB1 3AN
United Kingdom

info@windhorsepublications.com
www.windhorsepublications.com

Typeset and designed by Ben Cracknell Studios
Cover design by Deborah Harward
Cover image © James Thew
Printed by Bell & Bain Ltd, Glasgow

British Library Cataloguing in Publication Data:
A catalogue record for this book is available from the British Library

ISBN: 978 1 907314 93 3

Contents

About the author

Sangharakshita was born Dennis Lingwood in South London, in 1925. Largely self-educated, he developed an interest in the cultures and philosophies of the East early on, and realized that he was a Buddhist at the age of sixteen.

The Second World War took him, as a conscript, to India, where he stayed on to become the Buddhist monk Sangharakshita. After studying for some years under leading teachers from the major Buddhist traditions, he went on to teach and write extensively. He also played a key part in the revival of Buddhism in India, particularly through his work among followers of Dr B.R. Ambedkar.

After twenty years in India, he returned to England to establish the Friends of the Western Buddhist Order (FWBO) in 1967, and the Western Buddhist Order in 1968 (in 2010 the name of the FWBO was changed to the Triratna Buddhist Community, and that of the Order was changed to the Triratna Buddhist Order). Sangharakshita has always particularly emphasized the decisive significance of commitment in the spiritual life, the paramount value of spiritual friendship and community, the link between religion and art, and the need for a 'new society' supportive of spiritual aspirations and ideals.

In recent years Sangharakshita has been handing on most of his responsibilities to his senior disciples in the Order. From his base in Birmingham, he is now focusing on personal contact with people.

Acknowledgements

This is the second volume of Sangharakshita's commentary on Nāgārjuna's *Precious Garland*, promised when the first volume was published as *Living Ethically* in 2009. The commentary is based on a study seminar given by Sangharakshita in 1976, whose participants are to be thanked for the questions that prompted the reflections that now appear in this book.

If the seminar were to be held today, no doubt a digital recording would swiftly be made available on the excellent freebuddhistaudio.com. But, the product of an earlier age, the teaching is in your hands by virtue of arcane processes and cottage industries: sound recordists, transcribers, decipherers and typists, editors and proof-readers – an intensity of effort over many years that seems akin to the handing down of teachings in the early days of Buddhism. To all of them thanks are due.

The editing of the text is the inspired work of Tim Weston, Pabodhana and particularly Jinananda, a master of discernment and subtlety when it comes to the translation of the spoken word into prose, especially when the subject might seem to most people to be hard to fathom. And the text has come full circle, having been combed through by Sangharakshita himself, with the help of his secretary Vidyaruchi, and so in a sense being his most recent teaching.

But this is only one of many intersecting circles. The seminar was made possible by the translation of the text by Jeffrey Hopkins and Lati Rimpoche with Anne Klein, to whom many thanks are due. In this book we have quoted not the most recent edition (published by Snow Lion in 2007), but the one published by Harper & Row in 1975, on which the seminar was based. Our gratitude must of course include Nāgārjuna himself for his original text, described in *Living Ethically* as 'succinct, comprehensive, inspiring, a masterpiece of Mahayana expository literature'. And Nāgārjuna, in its very first verse, bows down to the Buddha ... We have chosen to begin *Living Wisely* on that note of gratitude and end it with transference of merits, for the perfection of wisdom is traditionally, and truly, seen in the context of devotion.

In the preface to *Living Ethically*, I ventured that 'perhaps the second volume could be considered to be revisiting the themes of the first viewed from a different level or perspective'. 'Beneath the question of how best to help others, and how to develop the altruistic spirit that wants to,' I said, 'are questions of another kind: what is 'self', what are 'others', and how does a world in which that distinction exists come into being?' In *Living Wisely*, such questions are tackled head on, not as abstruse brainteasers but as though they really matter – as indeed they profoundly do, if we really are to learn to live wisely.

To end on a note of gratitude, thanks are also due to Michelle Bernard and all at Windhorse Publications for all their work to make these teachings available for the benefit of all beings.

Vidyadevi
Herefordshire, August 2012

Introduction

The doctrines of definite goodness are
Said by the Conquerors to be deep,
Subtle and frightening to
Children who are not learned.[1]

The *Ratnamālā* or *Precious Garland* is a long sequence of verses in which the second-century Buddhist monk Nāgārjuna explains to an unknown king how to make progress on the spiritual path. In the first set of verses, 'High Status and Definite Goodness', Nāgārjuna outlines the practices that produce what he calls 'high status', by which he means rebirth in a state of happiness within *saṃsāra* as a human being or a god. Following this is a longer and more detailed account of the wisdom by means of which one achieves 'definite goodness'. By 'definite goodness' Nāgārjuna means liberation and omniscience, and by wisdom he means the cognition of emptiness, as described in the Perfection of Wisdom sūtras. Then, in the second section, 'An Interwoven Explanation of Definite Goodness and High Status', he explores at length the doctrinal basis for the attainment of spiritual

> Even the most learned adults are likely to be frightened by these doctrines.

insight, and discusses the nature of emptiness. Insight being so difficult to achieve, however, Nāgārjuna recommends to the king that he should apply himself to the wholehearted practice of ethics, which eventually is sure to lead him to wisdom.

Nāgārjuna's advice to the king on ethical matters was the theme of the first volume of this commentary, published as *Living Ethically*. This second volume goes on to consider the verses of the *Ratnamālā* that deal with teachings on wisdom and emptiness, which Nāgārjuna calls doctrines of 'definite goodness'. This shifts the emphasis away from high status within *saṃsāra* towards liberation from *saṃsāra* altogether. In this endeavour we need guidance from those who are themselves liberated: the Buddhas, or to use an equivalent term, Jinas or 'Conquerors'.

The Buddha remarked more than once in the course of his teaching life that the doctrines he was attempting to communicate were deep and subtle. Indeed, according to the Pāli scriptures, this was on his mind immediately after his Enlightenment, when he was considering whether to teach at all. He reflected that 'this Dharma, this truth, this reality which I have realized is deep, profound,'[2] meaning that it could not be understood on a purely rational level; indeed, that it could not be fully comprehended at any level by anyone who was not Enlightened. He was thinking in that context about the doctrine of conditioned co-production, but the same reservations could apply to teachings about liberation in general. However deeply you may go into them, absorbing them at ever more profound levels of your being, there are always more things to learn, deeper and broader ramifications to consider.

When the Buddha was wondering how to communicate the Dharma, he thought at first that it was too 'subtle' (*nipuṇa* in Pāli) to be made known to people whose minds were caught up in mere reasoning. Not that it is subtle in the intellectual sense; it is more that it is elusive. Eventually, of course, he saw that it could be communicated to those 'with little dust in their eyes'. The Dharma is not only subtle and profound. It is also frightening, though not – as the translation of this verse rather clumsily has it – simply to 'children who are not learned'. There is an antithesis here, as in the *Dhammapada*, between 'the fool' (*bāla*) and 'the wise' (*paṇḍita*). It is not lack of learning that renders the doctrines of definite goodness frightening, but immaturity – more precisely, spiritual immaturity. Likewise, if a 'pandit' is wise, it is not because he is learned. Where you are on the spectrum of spiritual maturity has nothing to do with intellectual acuity or learning or even how mature you are in the ordinary sense. Even the most learned adults are likely to be frightened by these doctrines. Why they might be so fearful, or even terrible, we shall be in a better position to understand when we look more closely at them.

Nāgārjuna sees this subtle wisdom as a middle way between extremes, for which reason the school he founded is known as the Madhyamaka, one of the two main schools of Mahāyāna philosophy. The other school is that of the Yogācāra. Nāgārjuna based his teachings on the *Perfection of Wisdom* sūtras, which he is said to have obtained from the nāgas, the wise serpent kings, and brought back from their palace in the depths of the ocean.[3] This mythic origin reflects the fact that they come from the very depths of human understanding, and in the Indo-Tibetan tradition, the Madhyamaka is always described as the 'profound Madhyamaka'. The Yogācāra on the other hand is described as the 'sublime Yogācāra', and again, the description is appropriate to the myth of its provenance, because the inspiration for the teaching is said to have come from above. Asaṅga, the founder of the school, is supposed to have ascended in meditation to the *tuṣita devaloka*, the heaven of content. There he received his inspiration from the Bodhisattva Maitreya, who waits in the Tuṣita heaven for the time to come when he will be reborn on earth for the last time and become a Buddha. As the teachings of the Yogācāra are said to have been brought back 'from on high' in this way, they are described as sublime.[4] The terms sublime and profound refer respectively to the heights and the depths of our experience; but these outer limits in either direction bring us to essentially the same realm of experience, one that is as far from our everyday understanding as it is possible to get. The teachings they describe come from another dimension; they are unimaginable to the mundane mind.

Chapter One

The relationship between wisdom and faith

I bow down to the all-knowing,
Freed from all defects,
Adorned with all virtues,
The sole friend of all beings.[5]

The Madhyamaka tradition is renowned for the relentlessness of its logic and for the subtlety with which it is able, from the perspective of *śūnyatā* (emptiness), to undermine all concepts, all notions of a stable or concrete reality. It may come as a surprise, therefore, to find that Nāgārjuna begins his treatise with an expression of heartfelt devotion to the Buddha. There is nothing intellectual about this opening verse at all. In hailing the Buddha as an exemplar of virtue and of wisdom, and a friend to all beings, Nāgārjuna is establishing a devotional, emotional rapport between himself and the Buddha. The word 'adorned' is particularly significant, emphasizing as it does that the Buddha's virtues are beautiful and attractive. For many people the word 'virtue' may suggest something rather grim and forbidding, but Nāgārjuna reminds us that

> Faith is not so much belief as a heartfelt response to the spiritually attractive.

true virtue is not like that at all. Seen as adorned with virtues, the Buddha becomes beautiful and fascinating, and this vision is the beginning of faith, in the sense of a heartfelt response to the spiritually attractive.

As he contemplates the Buddha, Nāgārjuna feels a *joy* that gathers in emotional intensity as the verse progresses. Beginning with the purely 'intellectual' category of 'all-knowing', and then praising the apparently negative characteristic that the Buddha is free from defects of character, Nāgārjuna goes on to see the Buddha as manifestly adorned with positive spiritual qualities, and as 'the sole friend of all beings'.

According to Aristotle friendship is a virtue, and therefore only the virtuous can be true friends.

Of all the superlatives in the verse, the final claim is perhaps the most surprising, suggesting as it does that only the Buddha can give us the help we truly need, so that he is the only real friend that any of us have. In other words, there is a link between virtue and friendship. Western philosophers would agree: Aristotle, for example, maintains that there can be no real friendship between those who are wicked. According to him, friendship is a virtue, and therefore only the virtuous can be true friends.[6]

How is this? What moral virtue and friendship have in common is an element of consistency and constancy. There may sometimes be a camaraderie amongst the wicked, but rarely is there true 'honour among thieves', and rarely therefore any real friendship between them. Without a high level of moral integrity, a person is always at the mercy of his or her own weaknesses and is therefore not dependable. In the normal run of things, most of us come to realize that there are certain people upon whom we can depend for most things and in most circumstances, while other people are likely to let us down when we are in trouble. It can be a distressing experience to learn that some of your 'friends' were only there for the good times; but it is comforting, on the other hand, to find out who your real friends are.

Ultimately, however, you can place complete trust only in someone whose virtues are solid enough to survive any change in circumstances whatsoever. The Buddha has this rock-like quality, but one who is full of kindness and concern as the result, say, of some temporary success in meditation may become rather less friendly when their meditation practice is less rewarding. Expressions of friendliness based upon positivity gained from meditation are certainly more reliable than protestations of eternal friendship made while in a state of alcoholic intoxication, say, but they are conditioned, nevertheless. The friendship of the Unconditioned mind, on the other hand, can be trusted absolutely. A Buddha may express himself in ways that are not what you expect or even welcome, but you can nonetheless entrust your ultimate welfare to him and his teaching. Likewise, the spiritual community, by virtue of its connection with transcendental ideals, can be broadly trusted to provide you with what you need, even if it is not always what you want.

It might even be said that one can be a true friend only to the extent that one has a spiritual life, in the broadest sense, in which case one's commitment is primarily to the ideal, and secondarily to one's friend. This order of priorities might seem to be a restriction of friendship, making it dependent on something that is outside it. But this would be to misunderstand the nature of the spiritual ideal, which is essentially about freedom and spontaneity. Only on the basis of that ideal of freedom and spontaneity can you commit yourself to a friendship in a truly positive way. You do not commit yourself to your friend in the sense of committing yourself to the various imperfections of their character. The basis of the relationship and what makes that mutual commitment possible is your shared commitment to your ideals.

Of course, many people haven't even heard of the Buddha. How, then, can he be a friend to all beings? He can be in the sense that he is potentially, or in principle, the friend of all beings inasmuch as through his teaching he gives them the greatest of all gifts, the gift of the Dharma.

When Nāgārjuna calls the Buddha the 'all-knowing', can we take him literally, or does he simply mean that he is completely Enlightened? The Sanskrit term being translated is not *samyak-sambuddha*, 'completely enlightened', but *sarva-jña*, 'omniscient', so it would seem that Nāgārjuna does indeed mean 'all-knowing'.

Someone who is spiritually enlightened may very well be entirely ignorant about quite a number of things, although this is something some people find it difficult to believe.

In the time of the Buddha there were teachers who claimed to know literally everything; or at least their disciples made this claim on their behalf. One such teacher was Mahāvīra,[7] the founder of Jainism, who in the Pāli scriptures is called Nātaputta. For example, he was said to know the exact number of leaves on any particular tree. Some people of the Buddha's time seem to have thought of Enlightenment in this way, as being a complete factual knowledge about everything that exists. However, the Buddha said quite clearly that he did not possess this kind of knowledge. He was not all-knowing in the sense that he literally knew everything. All he claimed was that he knew *nirvāna* and the path leading to *nirvāna*, and he knew what helped and what hindered one as one sought to follow that path. In other words, the Buddha's was a spiritual omniscience, and this is what Nāgārjuna means when he salutes him as *sarva-jña*.

After his Enlightenment the Buddha declares that he has seen the 'builder of the house'. He has seen, in other words, that the world as we experience it, with its problems and disappointments, is the illusory creation of an illusory idea of a fixed self. It is in *this* sense that the Buddha knows everything that there is to be known. He knows the *true nature* of all things. He also knows how illusory any kind of knowledge – except this direct cognizance of reality – really is. The Buddha's all-seeing knowledge is not concerned with the objects of ego-consciousness so much as with knowledge of what that ego-consciousness really amounts to.

Some Buddhist texts, particularly those of the Mahāyāna, out of devotion ascribe to the Buddha much more knowledge than he claimed to possess. Indeed, in some quarters the idea that a spiritual teacher should be all-knowing still persists. In India, for example, people sometimes go to their spiritual teacher with a stomach-ache expecting him to know precisely what is wrong and what they should do about it; and some Indian teachers do their best to live up to this expectation and offer answers to such questions in a very confident manner. What with all the competition, they are under pressure to adopt such a role; if they don't, there are other teachers who will. However, although it is comforting to think that you are in the hands of someone who knows everything, from the spiritual point of view it simply isn't necessary to have such a teacher. Someone who is spiritually enlightened may very well be entirely ignorant about quite a number of things, although this is something some people find it difficult to believe.

The Buddha would have known less about geography than most children of today. If he had considered the matter at all, he would presumably have thought that the world he lived in was dominated by a great central mountain called Mount Sumeru, rising out of the ocean and surrounded by seven mountain ranges, this being the traditional Indian view. In fact, it is hard for us to imagine how limited

Even supposing for a moment that the Buddha had indeed anticipated the theory of relativity, say, or quantum physics, this would not prove he was Enlightened.

was the range of information available to the Buddha. We do not, therefore, have to subscribe to what the Buddha may have thought about geography, or any of the other physical sciences, in order to gain insight into the nature of reality. By the same token, the Buddha's limited grasp of matters that we take for granted does not affect his spiritual knowledge in the least.

In other words, spiritual realization is quite compatible with scientific ignorance, and when the one is expressed through the medium of the other, it is important to distinguish between the two, and not to feel that in order to benefit from the teaching we have to swallow the scientific ignorance with it. Some modern Buddhists try to find in the scriptures teachings that seem to anticipate the discoveries of modern science, but this is entirely to misunderstand the nature of spiritual and transcendental knowledge. Even supposing that the Buddha had indeed anticipated the theory of relativity, say, or quantum physics, this would not prove he was Enlightened.

A Buddha, for example, would know that a motor car was conditioned, and he would not therefore be attached to it; but he wouldn't necessarily be able to tell you how it worked. In other words, he could have a deep spiritual understanding of the motor car without any mechanical understanding of it whatsoever. The two kinds of knowledge are entirely distinct. The Buddha would be seeing the motor car in its reality, but in another sense he would know nothing about it. He would know only that it was part of conditioned existence.

To appeal to science on behalf of Buddhism is basically to appeal to authority. In the modern world not everyone accepts authority of the religious kind, but a great deal of trust is placed in the authority of science. The scientist is the person who knows: science by very definition is knowledge; so if Buddhism agrees with science – or so the argument goes – Buddhism must be in the right. If a scientist speaks in favour of the spiritual life or Buddhism or meditation, that will enhance their standing in the eyes of many people. People from traditional Buddhist cultures seem to be particularly keen on presenting Buddhism in science-friendly terms. Conscious of the waning prestige of Buddhism in their country, they try to make a case for the congruence of their faith with science. In so doing, they may imagine that they are thereby strengthening Buddhism, but what they are really doing is submitting the spiritual authority of the Dharma to what they see – or imagine other people may see – as the greater authority of science.

Similar claims have been made on behalf of the ancient Indian wisdom of the Vedas. Hindus will sometimes say that if you only look deeply enough into the *Rigveda*, you will find all the instructions you need in order to build a nuclear device. They will tell you in all seriousness that the ancient Indians knew how to make atom bombs, but simply chose not to do so. Again, it is as though science was the real authority. But this is to tread on dangerous ground. Science, after all, is always changing: the science of today is not the science of yesterday, nor will it be the science of tomorrow. It is not as though there is an absolutely established body of scientific truth that everyone can accept. More importantly, any appeal on behalf of a spiritual tradition to scientific or any other authority comes from being unsure of one's ground, which in turn is likely to come from having little or no spiritual experience of one's own to fall back on. There is a more general misunderstanding at work here too: the assumption that spiritual knowledge is related in some way to mundane knowledge, that someone who studies philosophy or comparative religion is more likely to be able to understand the truths of Buddhism than someone who is a gardener or a window cleaner. But Buddhism can only be understood by virtue of spiritual insight, and spiritual insight has nothing to do with intellectual understanding.

> The English poet cannot just leave the flower growing where it is. He has to pluck it out, roots and all, and subject it to his musings on the nature of God and man.

It is even possible that the more highly educated and intellectual a person is, the less likely they will be able fully to appreciate – really to take in – the essence of Buddhism as a felt experience. They may be able to master the philosophical teachings and even write about them, though without sufficient spiritual experience they are likely to become confused and miss the point. To be a Buddhist is to understand certain spiritual principles and do your utmost to put these into practice.

Any idea we have of knowing something carries a certain assumption about the true nature of the thing known, its relation to the knower, and the kind of knowledge achieved. A flower, for example, can be known in a certain way by dissecting and classifying it. But an equally valid and for most people much more rewarding kind of knowledge of the flower depends not upon recognizing its botanical species, but seeing in its impermanent beauty a reminder of universal impermanence, including one's own impermanence.

In his essay 'East and West',[8] D.T. Suzuki makes an interesting comparison between two poems, one by a Japanese Zen poet and the other by the nineteenth-century English poet Alfred, Lord Tennyson. The two poems are about the same subject: a flower growing in a wall. Suzuki remarks that whereas the Zen poet just contemplates the flower in the usual Zen way, the English poet cannot help taking hold of it, both literally and metaphorically:

Flower in the crannied wall,
I pluck you out of the crannies,
I hold you here, root and all, in my hand,
Little flower – but if I could understand
What you are, root and all, and all in all,
I should know what God and man is.[9]

According to Suzuki, this poem illustrates an attitude towards nature, and perhaps towards life in general, that is peculiarly Christian. The English poet cannot just leave the flower growing where it is. He has to pluck it out, roots and all, and subject it to his musings on the nature of God and man. Suzuki suggests that if Tennyson had simply allowed the flower to grow where it was while he contemplated it rather than yanking it out of the wall, he might have gained some insight into its nature. As it is, he gets nowhere. Suzuki's point is well made, but it has also to be said that English poetry tends to be more complex than Zen poetry, and one should be careful not to make assumptions about the poet's intentions. There is almost certainly an element of impersonation in the poem – that is, one should not identify the poem's viewpoint as being too precisely that of the poet. In view of the richness of the poetic tradition in which Tennyson was writing, it seems probable that the irony and pathos of this collision of the philosopher and the scientist over the flower would not have been lost on him.

So from a spiritual point of view, how much intellectual knowledge of the Dharma do we need? The simple answer is: probably a lot less than we think. However, the role that study plays in our practice can owe as much to temperament as to necessity. Buddhism traditionally makes a distinction between what is termed the *dhammānusārin*, the 'doctrine follower', and the *saddhānusārin*, the 'faith follower', and it seems that people belong to one or the other of these types. For the faith follower, personal contact with the teacher is much more important than study. Faith followers are not inclined to bother with studying the Dharma much beyond the personal precepts and instructions that their teacher gives them; they are not concerned to learn more than a few basic principles that they can put into practice personally. The doctrine follower, by comparison, wants to know all about Buddhism in all its aspects, perhaps not even just the doctrines of their own school, and they are therefore not so dependent on the teacher. They like to work things out for themselves, and to find out what other people have thought and said and done in other times and other cultures.

> One cannot speak of wisdom in terms either of 'knowing' or of 'feeling'. It is both.

Both types of person are capable of practising Buddhism, inasmuch as both are 'followers': they both follow the Dharma in the sense of trying to be true to it, although in very different ways. The doctrine follower is much more than a mere intellectual or scholar, just as the faith follower is more than a sentimental devotee of the Buddha. If we seek examples of each type, the Buddha's companion Ānanda comes to mind as representative of the faith follower, while another of the Buddha's most famous disciples, Śāriputra, is clearly a doctrine follower. In the context of Tibetan Buddhism, if Je Tsongkhapa is very much the doctrine follower, Milarepa is equally obviously the faith follower.

The two approaches do not seem to combine naturally in the same person, and most people are clearly either one or the other. You might find yourself switching from one type to the other at different times in your life, but you are unlikely to be able to combine them fully at the same time, though you can do your best to balance out your main tendency. Doctrine followers at their best have broad sympathies, while faith followers at their best are deep and intense. The risk for doctrine followers is that they may become too wide in their sympathies, spreading themselves too thinly and thus becoming shallow in their practice. Meanwhile, faith followers run the risk of becoming too narrow, even a little fanatical, and unable to understand people with very different ways of practising the Dharma. To guard against such risks, all you can do is to make time for study if you have strong faith and devotion, or balance your predilection for learning, if that is the case, with devotional practice.

But even for the faith follower, a basic level of intellectual understanding is indispensable to spiritual progress, and this is something Nāgārjuna goes on to illustrate later in the *Precious Garland*. It is not enough to store up merit by making offerings to shrines and stūpas, by chanting the sacred scriptures, or even by moral action. You have to engage with the deeper truth of things, and this must involve the intellect as well as the emotions, wisdom as well as faith. Ultimately we are looking for a quality of wisdom that supersedes conventional understanding. The term wisdom is therefore open to misunderstanding if it is distinguished from faith in too rigid a way. Wisdom is not a cognitive as distinct from an emotional faculty. One cannot speak of wisdom in terms either of 'knowing' or of 'feeling'. It is both, once it is experienced at a high enough level. It is an intuitive understanding and also an intuitive feeling. In other words, at a higher level there is no real distinction between faith and wisdom, or devotion and understanding. They are not experienced separately or even jointly. It is comparable to the experience of being deeply engaged in a conversation. You are thinking and feeling at the same time, and it is not possible to distinguish between the two: the thought is the feeling and the feeling is the thought. The attainment of wisdom is like this, albeit at a much higher level.

So Nāgārjuna's aim in the *Precious Garland* is not to generate an *understanding* of the Dharma in the king, but to generate the Dharma itself, just as the Buddha is described not as speaking about the Dharma, but as speaking Dharma. Nāgārjuna doesn't want to talk *about* the truth. He wants to *awaken* the truth. He is reminding the king of his inherent potential for Enlightenment, for establishing the practices and becoming thereby a vessel of the Dharma.

> *Through faith one relies on the practices,*
> *Through wisdom one truly knows,*
> *Of these two, wisdom is the chief,*
> *Faith is its prerequisite.*[10]

To summarize this verse: it is through faith that you are able to commit yourself to the practices and it is through the practices that you achieve high status. It is then through wisdom that you attain definite goodness and break the hold on your mind of the desire for happiness and high status.

Nāgārjuna's interpretation of faith here seems to be pitched at quite a low level; he seems to be suggesting that it is relatively unimportant compared with wisdom. It is true that the word 'wisdom' implies intellectual cognition, and by definition gives the emotional side of things less emphasis. But to think of it in this way is to miss the heart of the matter. To understand the true relationship between faith and wisdom we do well to consider the teaching of the five spiritual faculties.[11] Here, faith and wisdom are equal and coordinate, each balancing the other, without any suggestion that faith is somehow less important than wisdom. Following this teaching, one cannot say that wisdom is the 'chief' over faith any more than faith is the 'chief' over wisdom. One might just as well say that wisdom is the prerequisite of faith as that faith is the prerequisite of wisdom.

When it is linked with wisdom, faith is a total emotional response to the spiritual ideal.

But many modern Buddhist writers, especially Theravādins, share Nāgārjuna's emphasis here. One sign of this is the translation of *śraddhā* as 'confidence'. Confidence is certainly one level of *śraddhā*'s meaning, and faith at this level, as Nāgārjuna says, enables you to rely on the practices. But it is not the whole meaning of faith, because ultimately the wisdom through which you achieve definite goodness needs to be balanced with a higher faith. When it is linked with wisdom, faith is a total emotional response – even an aesthetic response – to the spiritual ideal, to the virtues with which the Buddha is adorned. It includes confidence and trust, but there is also a strong element of devotion. For Nāgārjuna, faith in this sense is generally every bit as important as wisdom, so perhaps here he should be paraphrased as follows: It is through confidence that one comes to rely on the practices, which will then bring about the arising of wisdom joined with faith, by which 'one truly knows'. Of these two, wisdom joined with faith is the chief, and confidence secondary, even though confidence is needed in order to bring the higher spiritual quality of wisdom/faith into being.

He who does not neglect the practices
Through desire, hatred, fear or ignorance
Is known as one of faith, a superior
Vessel for definite goodness.[12]

You need faith if you are to lead the spiritual life. It is through faith that undermining and distracting emotions such as craving, hatred, and fear are overcome. Faith is also needed to counteract spiritual ignorance, by which I mean an essentially emotional resistance to spiritual practice under the guise of a pseudo-objective depreciation of its value. It is possible to hold these negative states at bay temporarily in meditation, and thus to enjoy a deeper state of absorption and concentration, and no doubt faith at a very basic level is required if we are to practise meditation in this way. However, a much deeper faith is needed in order to commit oneself to a path of practice that promises to destroy the very roots of those negative states. Faith does not come on its own. It is connected with refined positive emotions such as friendliness, compassion, joy and equanimity (the four *brahma-vihāras*)[13] and also with devotion. To these one can add the positive counterparts of the hindrances to meditation: contentment, patience, energy and concentration. Without these qualities little spiritual progress can be made. You may want to be free of negative emotions, but you cannot just push them away; they must be replaced with something more positive.

> If there's no joy in your spiritual life, there's no faith either. Without joy, there may be belief, but no faith.

The immediate benefit that we can expect from Buddhist practice is not that it will make us happier and more contented or even psychologically healthy, at least not in the way that we normally think of these qualities. What we can hope for is that it will help us to be more emotionally positive, though in a refined sense. Taking up Buddhism should help us become more interested in other people, more able to empathize with them, more willing to rejoice in other people's happiness, and less likely to fall into states of dejection or elation as the result of everyday circumstances. Above all, it should bring us a joy that is not dependent upon ordinary human happiness or contentment.

In very simple terms faith is a deep enjoyment of the contemplation of the ideal. As Nāgārjuna says in an earlier verse of the *Precious Garland*, faith is the 'quintessence of the means' of happiness. When you contemplate the Buddha-ideal, or the figure of the historical Śākyamuni, and experience a deep happiness, that is faith. Faith means rejoicing in your practice and being fascinated by the spiritual ideal, which in itself will make you want to get on with your practice. Rejoicing in the Buddha's qualities, you will feel happy, and getting on with your spiritual practice is a natural expression of that happiness. In this way you are carried along in your practice by your faith. So faith is not mere belief in this or that doctrine; it is a response of delight and fascination, much more like one's emotional response to a beautiful painting or piece of music or landscape.

Faith is not a sort of investment plan. You're not putting in a lot of laborious practice in the belief that you will reap dividends later on. It may be necessary at a very early stage to grit your teeth and carry on regardless, but you should not accept that this is just the way things are. You should always be looking to emerge into a feeling of happiness about what you are doing. If there's no joy in your spiritual life, there's no faith either. Without joy, there may be belief, but no faith.

In simple terms, Buddhist faith may be said to consist in rejoicing in the Buddha's full realization of his spiritual potential, and trusting that you yourself are capable of reaching the same goal. By contrast, John Middleton Murry, writing about Cardinal Newman, observed that the cardinal believed in God but did not trust him.[14] This must be terrible: to have a firm belief that your fate is in the hands of someone who cannot be trusted to look after you! You can never be quite sure whether your wretched accumulation of virtues is going to see you through or whether some long-forgotten unconfessed sin may not trip you up and cast you straight down into hell. Even if you have forgotten it, you can be sure that the vengeful Jehovah of the Old Testament has not. Believing in God is like having an angry father; you know he's there, and you don't trust him not to turn round and give you a theophanic clip round the ear from time to time. At the very least, our Christian conditioning may encourage us to think of the spiritual life as essentially sweat, grind and struggle, and this is no basis for the arising of faith in the true sense of the term.

These Old Testament attitudes are very often the aspects of Christianity that linger in the post-Christian consciousness, and they seep into the ways in which some Western people relate to Buddhism. Of course there is more to Christianity than this. One has only to look around medieval cathedrals, listen to the best of Christian devotional music, or read the words of the King James Bible, to get some sense that there is a healthier kind of Christian faith, based on an awareness of what the Bible calls 'the beauty of holiness'. Nor can we say that Buddhism is all sweetness and light. Clearly the Dharma poses a threat to the ego, and to have to confront the reality of *śūnyatā* can be terrifying (even though the threat holds no danger because it threatens what in any case is unreal).

In one of the Mahāyāna sūtras Ānanda is asked what initially attracted him to Buddhism, and he says that it was the personal appearance of the Buddha. When he saw a beautiful light

> Believing in God is like having an angry father; you know he's there, and you don't trust him not to turn round and give you a theophanic clip round the ear from time to time.

shining from the Buddha's body – the radiance of all his past meritorious deeds – he was so overwhelmed that he simply had to become a disciple.[15] For him it was an aesthetic as much as a spiritual experience. However, with all its disciplines and restrictions, religious faith and practice is often regarded in the West as being rather unattractive, even grim and forbidding. I remember that on my return to England in the 1960s I led a celebration of the festival of Wesak, the anniversary of the Buddha's attainment of Enlightenment, at the invitation of the London Buddhist Society. As I gave my little talk, I couldn't help noticing how glum everyone seemed at the idea that the Buddha had attained Enlightenment and shown them the path to *nirvāṇa*. They seemed rather sorry that he had gone to all that trouble! By contrast, in early Buddhist scriptures like the *Mahāvastu*,[16] the whole text is suffused with an atmosphere of rejoicing in the Buddha. Everybody is happy that a Buddha has arisen in the world. It is almost as though life has become one great long celebration.

The Buddhists I encountered at that Wesak meeting in London were very different from the monks I had known in the East. A Buddhist monk is supposed to have given up everything. He has no home, no wife, no job. And yet even the oldest and most infirm of them is cheerful and even jolly much of the time. Contrary to popular belief, not all monks are highly spiritual people, devoting their time to silent meditation or study of the sūtras. They are by no means otherworldly. Yet they do not chafe at the life of renunciation. In freeing them from worldly attachments, it leaves them happy and carefree, like schoolboys on holiday. Even if they do not experience deep compassion, they generally feel sorry for lay people, with their worldly cares and responsibilities. Renunciation even seems to keep them young. A layman of 50 may be beginning to show his years, but a monk of the same age often looks quite boyish.

If there is one thing above all others that is lacking in Western Buddhism it is perhaps the atmosphere of joy that we find in the older Buddhist texts and in traditional Buddhist societies. We could start to remedy this by celebrating traditional Buddhist festivals in a more colourful and joyful manner. After all, the spiritual life is a happy life. If you cannot be happy following the spiritual path and living in accordance with the Dharma, how are you ever going to be happy? Buddhism may not be easy, but even at its most difficult, it should certainly not be miserable.

This is a constant theme in the *Songs of Milarepa*. The Tibetan yogi Milarepa lived a life of extreme physical hardship, but communicated his joy in the Dharma through his songs. One of the stories about Milarepa describes a young man who, even as he is reduced to suicidal despair by Milarepa's initial refusal to take him on as a disciple, declares 'I have never been so happy as today.'[17] The spiritual life is sometimes like that: you may be experiencing real suffering, and at the same time you have never been so happy in your life. This is happiness in a deeper sense than mere pleasurable feeling – it is the happiness that comes from faith. The way of life to which this faith leads you may sometimes be difficult, but you know in your heart of hearts that you are on the right track.

Chapter Two

....

The essence of the matter

'I am not, I will not be.
I have not, I will not have',
That frightens all children
And kills fear in the wise.[18]

The doctrine of definite goodness is what we might call Buddhism proper, or the true Dharma. This is the essence of the matter: no 'I', and therefore no 'mine'. What we experience as the 'I', what we experience as 'myself', is not an ultimately real entity. There is, therefore, no question of 'me' as I experience myself being really and truly here, either in the present or in the future. Since there is in reality no 'me' in the ultimate sense, there is no question of my possessing anything, either now or later on: 'I have not, I will not have.' No self, no possessions.

Why should the waking consciousness proclaim the 'I' as the totality of our existence? We are more than that, bigger, more multi-faceted.

The ordinary person will take this as meaning 'You simply don't exist', and that must surely be seen as a very terrible thing. This is meant to be the path of liberation, but when they first come across this teaching, very few people are going to experience it as being liberating. It is natural to feel that it negates one's whole being, and this is very difficult to accept. The doctrine of definite goodness spells the death of the ego, and when we realize that the ego is pretty well everything with which we identify, it feels like *our* death. However, what the doctrines are really pointing out is that what you take for reality, that is to say yourself, is not the be-all and end-all of existence that you take it for. It is not that you are completely non-existent or unreal. It is rather that you do not exist in the way you think you do. There is another dimension of your experience that is more real, and in contrast with this reality, what you take to be real is an illusion. Indeed, far from being a threat, to the wise this doctrine 'kills fear'. All fear, after all, arises out of one's desire to preserve and protect the ego. But if the ego is shown to be an illusion, one's fears on its behalf are extinguished. You see that there is no one to lose anything, and so you have nothing to lose. If you have no 'I', you save yourself a world of trouble.

This may sound simple, and in fact it *is* simple, but getting a real sense of it is not. It is subtle and elusive. Sometimes you may get a fleeting glimpse of it at the moment of waking. Perhaps you catch the tail-end of a dream and realize that for what seems like hours you have been living some other life in some other world or dimension. Because it has so little connection with your daily life, it slips away from you almost immediately, but at such times you may get the feeling that there is another life behind your normal waking existence. It is easy to forget this other life, but we return to it again and again when we dream; and while we are in it, we identify with it just as we identify with our daily life. In the Indian tradition generally, though perhaps more within the Vedic tradition than in Buddhism, it is customary to reflect upon the fact that we have another existence in the world of dreams. This other dimension of consciousness is regarded as being as real in its own way as our 'normal' waking experience.

Within Tibetan Buddhism, 'dream yoga', one of the six yogas of Nāropa, is an attempt to prolong awareness into the dream state, so that you dream consciously and learn to direct your dreams.[19] Eventually this practice awakens you to the fact that waking consciousness is only the tip of an iceberg. You spend hours every night dreaming – so where do you go, what do you do? Is your dream life not part of your life? Does it not have an effect upon your state of mind?

The Vedic tradition attaches particular importance to the state of dreamless sleep. No object is experienced, and therefore the ego is not experienced either, so deep sleep is regarded as a kind of unconscious or negative state of union with Brahman. From a Buddhist point of view, however, it is not a state of real Insight or Enlightenment, because there is no awareness in it, neither waking consciousness nor dream consciousness, and with the reawakening of consciousness from the state of deep sleep the ego returns. Nor do you remember anything of that state of deep dreamless sleep. However, it certainly provides daily evidence for the fact that the mind is not limited to ordinary waking consciousness. It has other dimensions, which we play down because they seriously undermine the claims of the waking self to be the whole of us. But why should the waking consciousness appropriate our total being? Why should it proclaim the 'I' as the totality of our existence? We are more than that, bigger, more multi-faceted.

People who have experimented with consciousness-altering drugs tend to be more aware of these other realms of being than most people. Although they will not have entered them with either discipline or consistency, they have nevertheless had a direct experience of the fact that what we normally think of as the finite human personality is only a very small part of what is actually there. In meditation we have the opportunity to enter into further levels or dimensions of mind in a more integrated and sustained way. People who are not very imaginative are often bemused by the ability of those who have a cultivated or creative inner life to enjoy themselves without many material rewards or satisfactions. Anyone who meditates should be able, at least for a while, to live with even fewer of the material supports upon which the ego relies. Even if you lose everything – your money, your job, even your freedom – you know that you have inner resources upon which you can draw. You can still explore the infinite riches of your dream life, and the depths of your mind as revealed in meditation.

Not only is the 'I' only one small aspect of the self; it is one, moreover, that is constantly changing. As we realize the other dimensions that are accessible to us, we should be able to see that the ego, with all its petty anxieties and resentments, is not as important as it thinks it is. Otherwise, we confine ourselves to a narrow band of the total spectrum of our experience, as if the colour orange were to claim that it was the only colour, and that the other colours of the rainbow were somehow unreal or imagined. The ego is highly adaptable, of course, and will subtly appropriate experiences wherever it can do so. We have to be careful not to posit some kind of self-existent, absolutely real 'big self' to which we go forth from our 'small self'. However, reality can only be reached through an expansion of consciousness, through bringing all the bands of the whole spectrum of consciousness together, not by simply focusing on our present experience.

> By him who speaks only to help
> Beings, it was said that they all
> Have arisen from the conception of 'I'
> And are enveloped with the conception of 'mine'.[20]

Our conception of separate beings arises from the conception of 'I'. This is not to say that without the conception of 'I' you have non-being. Without the 'I' you have neither being nor non-being. The 'I' thought is the seed from which our sense of being arises. Enveloping this seed of being there is a wider conception of 'mine', representing the extent of its possessions. Here am I, sitting in the midst of my possessions: my house, my car, my land, my wife, my family, my football team, my religion. All my possessions act as a kind of tent protecting the conception of 'I', creating the little cocoon that is my world and that fills out the 'I', giving it a sense of solidity and permanence. 'I' and 'mine' are therefore very closely intertwined. The envelope protects, but it also limits. It is as though the 'I', the sense of self, sets an inner limit, while the sense of 'mine' sets an outer one.

> All my possessions act as a kind of tent protecting the conception of 'I', creating the little cocoon that is my world and that fills out the 'I', giving it a sense of solidity and permanence.

Nāgārjuna's designation of the Buddha as one who speaks only to help beings gives us an insight into the nature of the Enlightened mind. Even when he is asking someone to do something, as when he asks Meghiya to stay with him and not go and meditate, his own need for a companion is not at the forefront of his mind.[21] Likewise, even when he speaks of the non-existence of the ego or self, his message is one of compassion, loving kindness, and sympathetic joy. He is not out to deprive us of anything. Indeed, he is doing quite the opposite.

When considering these teachings, we have to be careful that we do not approach the Dharma with a negative self-view. If our gut-feeling is that we have or are a self, it can feel as if the Dharma is going to take something away from us that is central to who we are, when in fact the Dharma is there to help us see ourselves, whatever we may be, more clearly. Perhaps it is better simply to see ourselves as limited. Instead of challenging ourselves to explode our deluded conception of the self directly, it may be more helpful to think of breaking out of the closed circle of self-interest that is the emotional expression of our delusion. We can think of expanding that circle through the cultivation of *mettā* or loving kindness until our self-interest is absorbed in a concern for the welfare of all living beings.[22] Overcoming ego is not just an idea; it is an experience, a way of life.

'The "I" exists, the "mine" exists.'
These are wrong as ultimates,
For the two are not [established]
By a true and correct consciousness.[23]

The key phrase here is 'wrong as ultimates'. 'I' and 'mine' are real experiences, but they have only a provisional validity. Experience the 'I', acknowledge your possessions as your own, as 'mine', but don't take these notions as the last word on the subject; don't take these inner horizons as giving you any idea of the true extent of your mind, your world, your reality. Why? Because this is how the Enlightened consciousness, which sees things as they really are, experiences 'I' and 'mine': it sees them as only relatively real, not absolutely real. It expands beyond the 'I', the 'mine'. Growth is not just up; it is not just a two-dimensional development. It is in all directions. It is therefore not always very obvious. Sometimes you may feel as though you are not growing spiritually, but it may be that you are developing in ways, in directions, that you have not been able to envisage.

The mental and physical aggregates arise
From the conception of 'I' which is false in fact.
How could what is grown
From a false seed be true?[24]

The five aggregates (*skandhas*) are: *rūpa* (form), *vedanā* (feeling), *saññā* (Pāli)/*saṃjñā* (Sanskrit) (perception), *saṃskāra* (volition), and *viññāṇa* (Pāli)/*vijñāna* (Sanskrit) (consciousness). They make up the various constituents of the psycho-physical organism. When Nāgārjuna refers to what is grown from a false seed, he is referring to the traditional teaching that we are reborn out of ignorance. So again he employs an exclusively negative approach to the ego with a view to getting rid of it completely, at a stroke. It's as though he's not prepared to admit that there is any truth in the ego at all. But how are we to respond to this analysis creatively? Another way of looking at the mental and physical aggregates is to see them as representing a kind of concretization of the ego, a rather rigid structure, closed in on itself. Our task is to open this structure out.

The ego is a way of behaving, a kind of revolving upon your own axis. It is a particular kind of limitation placed upon experience.

Rather than trying to put the ego out of reckoning altogether, it may be better to change the way we see it, to see it less as a thing and more as a way of functioning, or a way of being.

The language we use can be less than helpful when it comes to the ego. Expressions like 'transcending the ego' create a lot of confusion by apparently fixing something non-existent in the form of an apparent object of knowledge. The result is nonsensical: we talk of getting rid of something that never existed or even denying this object of intense interest and concern any reality at all. 'The ego', we say, 'is not real.' If we're not careful, we can spend a lot of time talking about something that does not exist in such a way that it becomes more real to us than it was before we started making so much of it.

The ego doesn't exist even on an empirical or relative level, let alone as a real object of perfect wisdom. At the same time, the term refers to a genuine experience. We have habits of selfishness, and our task is to transform these habits. If we introduce an imaginary object called the ego or the 'I' into the discussion, we complicate the process unnecessarily. You are functioning as an 'ego' when you are closed in on yourself, when you shut yourself off from other people. When you are more outward-going and expansive, on the other hand, when you are engaging with the concerns of others, you are functioning from 'non-ego'. These are two very different experiences: one reactive, the other creative. In a reactive state you feel cold and hard, as though there's a tight little ball inside you, or as if you are constantly circling back on yourself. But in a creative state you feel free and open, expansive and flowing; instead of the little ball there is warmth, radiation, a spiralling outwards and upwards. Note that I am using the *image* of expanding and contracting, which like all images has to be understood properly. It is not that the ego is expanding or contracting. The ego is the contraction of one's being around a delusion, and non-ego is the expansion of one's being. But this expansion is not just inflation. It is a mode of action that does not feed or reinforce that delusion.

This gives us a way of working in accordance with our nature. As we know, sometimes we function in one way, sometimes in the other. If we can be aware of which function is operative at any one time, we are in a position to do something about it, either to sustain it or to break out of it. It is not as if there is a thing called 'ego' that we have to worry about 'having' and 'getting rid of'. It is rather that there is a more satisfying way of living. It may be that you do experience 'something': something hard, knotted and tight, something lodged like a billiard ball in your gullet. You may well feel you need somehow to vomit it up. But there's nothing actually there – that's the point. It is a snarl in a skein of wool, a tangle or knot. It just has to be loosened, opened, unravelled, not cut out. At the same time, that knot is a real knot. We can experience ourselves as ego, and that is a real experience. The ego is a way of behaving, a kind of revolving upon your own axis. It is a particular kind of limitation placed upon experience, a non-expansion or blockage of energy. This fact makes it possible to become free of it, here and now, by behaving in a non-egoistic way, by going out from yourself, by orbiting around something bigger than yourself. In this way you refine the ego out of existence.

Instead of saying that the ego does not exist or that it is not real, you could say instead that to be constantly turning in upon yourself is not the most satisfying form of existence. There are better options available to you. Instead of saying to yourself 'Just drop the ego', you can say, 'Let yourself open up a little' or even 'Let yourself go.' To the extent that you think of others with genuine concern, you are non-egoistic. Even if you are just thinking of your own wife and children, that is an important step towards being non-egoistic. Thinking about your family is certainly a more effective way of beginning to realize the truth of what Nāgārjuna is saying here than just reading about it and understanding it intellectually.

Paraphrasing Nāgārjuna's verse, we can say: 'Having seen that the egocentric way of behaving is not the best way in which one can behave, one abandons that way of behaving and embarks on a more expansive and other-regarding way of behaving.' As a result of that spiralling outwards of one's being, one's experience of oneself is no longer fixed, rigid and closed. That is, you become so expansive, so engaged with and interested in the needs of others, that the possibility of going back to that old constrained and self-regarding behaviour no longer exists. The process of your expansion has gathered such momentum that it is now irreversible. It is not that you have somehow jettisoned this thing called 'ego', this extra baggage you do not now need; it is simply that the whole momentum of your being is so creative, so outward-looking, that to behave selfishly has become impossible. It would be against your very nature, and as such quite perverse. This point is what is traditionally known in Buddhism as the point of Stream-entry.[25]

Chapter Three

Images of emptiness

Next, Nāgārjuna uses a sequence of images to express, or give some sense of, the nature of emptiness or *śūnyatā*: an empty mirror, a wheel of fire, and a mirage.

The empty mirror

Just as it is said
That an image of one's face is seen
Depending on a mirror
But does not in fact exist [as a face],

So the conception of 'I' exists
Dependent on the aggregates,
But like the image of one's face
In reality the 'I' does not exist.

Just as without depending on a mirror
The image of one's face is not seen,
So too the 'I' does not exist
Without depending on the aggregates.[26]

To see the reflection of your face, you need to look into a mirror. Without the mirror, there is no reflection. In this image Nāgārjuna is saying that it is the same with the *skandhas*. Due to their existence, you see in them an 'I', a self, and if they did not exist, the idea of a self could not arise. The fact of the matter is that you do have physical form, you do have consciousness, feeling, perceptions and volition, and it is on this basis that you are able to be aware of something

The ego does not exist as a thing, so it is not an object of consciousness, but a way of being conscious of things, a way of being, of behaving.

you think of as yourself. Of course it works the other way round as well: the *skandhas* arise from the conception of 'I'. It's a reciprocal relation, a mutual arising, but here just one side of it is emphasized.

In the case of the mirror, the reflection you see does not exist within the mirror. This idea of what you look like only arises in the way it does because you have looked into the mirror and interpreted what you see as you – which in a sense it is. But in another sense it is not you at all. The aggregates do not include the 'I', just as the mirror, as an object, does not include the reflection of the face. At the same time the aggregates are who you are in a truer sense than is the 'I'.

Your reflection in the mirror only arises upon the basis of the mirror being there to receive it. Likewise, the self you perceive when you become aware of physical form, feeling, perception, volition, and consciousness arises upon the basis of those five processes. Nāgārjuna is not suggesting that the aggregates are non-existent, any more than the mirror is non-existent. They represent a particular view of one's existence. The 'I' is an extreme version, a sort of concretization of that view.

The *skandhas*, like the elements, only exist, or possess an identity, due to their relationship with things other than themselves. The idea of 'form' only has meaning inasmuch as we are able to make a distinction between form and, say, feeling, or consciousness, and the same goes for the other aggregates. In each case, it is the activity of consciousness that enables us to make the distinction. Just as 'short' has no existence without 'tall', or cause without effect, the individual *skandhas* are no more substantial than is the illusory 'self' they appear to support.

Nāgārjuna's image of course has its limitations. The point to stress here is that the reflection of your face that you can see in the mirror is by no means the whole of you. It is a two-dimensional presentation of one aspect of you. All the other aspects of what you are – your dream life, your meditative experience, your memories of the past, your mindfulness, your ideals and aspirations, your relationships with others, and so on – are absent from that two-dimensional image. The mirror, like the *skandhas*, is itself dependent upon other factors for its existence. The reflection arises upon the basis of an object deployed as a mirror by an embodied intelligence with organs of vision. Likewise, the *skandhas* do not exist as separate objects apart from the intelligence that is trying to understand its own processes by means of them. This having been said, it must be emphasized that analogies between consciousness and an object of consciousness, however elusive – such as a reflection – are potentially very misleading. The ego does not exist as a thing, so it is not an object of consciousness, but a way of being conscious of things, a way of being, of behaving. Nor is it really even that. It is not an *it*, not *an* anything. The ego is like a reflection only in a very limited, specific sense.

Such images need to be understood in terms of what they might mean for us in quite practical, everyday ways. The question is not 'Do I have an ego or not?' but 'Am I looking out beyond what I already know, exploring new avenues, or am I simply going round the same old treadmill of my habits, my established views, my likes and dislikes? Am I stuck with a fixed idea of who and what I am?'

Nāgārjuna's starting point is the understanding that it is because we have an (imagined) ego to begin with that we are egoistic. But we can go a little further and say that because we can be egoistic we can also be altruistic or non-egoistic. If we develop Nāgārjuna's image on that basis we can say that the mirror can either reflect a face or reflect reality, which is empty. Both are possibilities for you, even if only one of them, the empty mirror, reflects you as you really are. Just as the same mirror can either reflect the face of the watcher or a world without fixed and permanent objects, so consciousness can either contract around a clearly defined 'self' in the limited sense or break out of that self-referential view of things. It can be reactive or creative, expansive or contracting, free or trapped. Imagine, say, looking in the mirror and seeing myriad facets of yourself, connecting you with everyone in the world, with everything in the universe. The empty mirror is an image for a consciousness that is not constrained by always referring to some static image of what you think you are.

> When the superior Ānanda[27] had
> Attained [insight into] what this means,
> He won the eye of doctrine[28] and taught it
> Continually to the monks.[29]

The energy it released in him could not be contained because it came out of the depths of his being. It co-existed with his life, and could not be switched off.

By 'superior' is meant something more like 'senior', and it probably translates the term sthavira. The 'eye of doctrine' is the *Dharmacakṣu*, the Dharma eye: the eye that sees the truth. To 'attain the eye of the Dharma' is a common idiom in the Pāli and Sanskrit scriptures. It means to develop this 'gnostic' spiritual faculty for the direct vision of truth. It is of course a non-dual vision; it is as if you see with a single eye. The result of this depth of Insight is that one feels impelled to teach other people how to gain Insight themselves. It is not like a job that you take on. When Ānanda had attained Insight into what Nāgārjuna calls the doctrines of definite goodness, he could not hold back from sharing it with others. The energy it released in him could not be contained because it came out of the depths of his being. It co-existed with his life, and could not be switched off. According to the available records, after the Buddha's *parinirvāṇa*, Ānanda gained full Enlightenment and had a large following, becoming revered almost as a second Buddha within his lifetime.

Bound upon a wheel of fire

There is misconception of an 'I' as long
As the aggregates are misconceived,
When this conception of an 'I' exists,
There is action which results in birth.[30]

You misconceive the aggregates of *rūpa, vedanā, saṃjñā, saṃskāra* and *vijñāna* when you think of them as static and unchanging things instead of processes of continual flux and transformation. It is when you start to experience what is essentially a process as something static that the 'I' comes into existence. But the 'I' that is aware that you are doing this

> Rebirth means in simple terms repeating old patterns and putting off being truly creative.

and starts to reverse the process is not quite the 'I' that is actually doing it, and this raises all sorts of mysterious and confusing questions. Who is it that gets rid of the ego? Who is it that gains Enlightenment? How can the ego get rid of itself? How do we get rid of something that doesn't exist? However, these are the sorts of question into which the Buddha did not think it useful to enquire. He simply said that when you reverse the process, when you stop trying to stem the flow, when you stop seeing the dynamic as static, then you will understand those things, and not before.

Birth considered as a result of action means in this context *re*-birth – that is, the repetition of an old pattern. When you try to arrest the flow, when you try to make what is dynamic into something static, you cannot prevent that dynamic process from going on, but you set up a patterning that gives an appearance of stasis. The continuing repetition of that pattern is what we call rebirth. Action that results in rebirth is habitual reaction rather than creative action. It expresses only the limitations inherent in that pattern. It is repeating the old patterning into another life, and that repetition reinforces the tendency to go on repeating the pattern. When this idea of an 'I' dominates consciousness, therefore, it leads to the arising through rebirth of a personality that is, in its significant aspects, very much like the old one. In simple terms rebirth means repeating old patterns and putting off being truly creative.

> With these three pathways mutually causing each
> Other without a beginning, middle or an end,
> This wheel of cyclic existence
> Turns like the 'wheel' of a firebrand.[31]

A firebrand whirled around in the hand produces the illusion of a circle or wheel of fire, a suggestive image for the wheel of cyclic existence, a world we see in terms of things that are in fact illusions formed out of repeated actions. The three pathways are presumably (though this is not completely clear) the misconception of the true nature of the skandhas, the misconception of an 'I' based on them, and the action of the 'I', which eventually results in rebirth. In other words, if you fail to see the aggregates in their true nature (i.e. as subject to the three lakṣaṇas) you will form the wrong conception of a 'self' or 'I', and the actions performed by this 'self' or 'I' will repeat the old pattern that has been set up. Because it has been repeated so often and, in a way, so successfully, it is virtually – though not quite – impossible to stop.

The 'three pathways' produce one another in a pattern of mutual causality. That is, none of them exists on its own, so that none of them is capable of beginning the process. Nor can you conceive of their beginning or ending. You are in the midst of it all, you are part of it, you *are* these pathways, so how can you see the beginning or end of them?

> *Because this wheel is not obtained from self, other*
> *Or from both, in the past, the present or the future,*
> *The conception of an 'I' ceases,*
> *And thereby action and rebirth.*[32]

This is hardly possible to explain; you either see it or you don't. The 'wheel is not obtained from self' because the self is part of the wheel. Similarly, it is not obtained from what is other than the self, or both from the self and the non-self, in the past, present or future, because these too are part of the wheel. The wheel doesn't arise in dependence upon anything else, and therefore it doesn't cease in dependence upon anything else either. This is important because it means that there is nothing outside the process, this endless going round, to bring it to a halt. The conception of an 'I' ceases when you see the whole wheel as being no more than a self-contained process. It is the self that perpetuates the illusion, and the self alone that is instrumental in its ceasing. The conception of an 'I' ceases when you see that there is no possibility of stepping outside your experience – the wheel – and being a self or 'I' who possesses that experience. Then of course there can be no action based upon the conception of 'I', and no rebirth.

The difficulty in communicating this idea is that one must speak as though the 'I' were real, since otherwise you cannot refer to 'it' at all. One traditional way of explaining this point is for the teacher to close his hand into a fist. When he opens his hand, what has happened to the fist? Does it still exist, or has it ceased to exist? Are the hand and the fist the same, or are they different? Are they both, or are they neither? Similarly, when you become Enlightened, what happens to your ego? It goes the same way as the fist. It is inappropriate to say that it continues to exist, that it does not continue to exist, or both, or neither. There was in reality no fist apart from the open hand you see now. Likewise, there never was an ego apart from the egoless reality that seemed to replace it, and that ego therefore never ceased to exist either. We can think of the open hand with its display of fingers as the aggregates. When the hand and fingers are closed up into a fist, then we have the ego. When the hand and fingers are opened, what has happened to the ego? Can you really say that the ego once existed but that now it does not? Can you say that the ego never existed, either then or now? Perhaps we should drop the idea of the fist and say that at first we saw a closed hand, and now we see an open one.

The problem of the illusory ego is to some extent linguistic. Something non-existent has the same nominative status as something real. Once it is named, even as being non-existent, it starts to play a syntactically substantive role. This unconscious sleight of hand is regularly exploited by the Zen masters. In one well-known story, the master asks the disciple, 'What are you carrying in your hand?' When the student replies that he is not carrying anything, the master says, 'Well then, put it down.' The illusory burden is of course the ego, the 'I'.

> *Thus one who sees how cause and effect*
> *Are produced and destroyed*
> *Does not regard the world*
> *As really existent or non-existent.*[33]

This verse is Nāgārjuna's summary of the difficult question of the non-existent ego. If it exists, how can you get rid of it? If it does not exist, how is it able to create so much trouble? The best course is to see things in terms of cause and effect: not as things that are produced and destroyed but as interlinked processes, emerging in dependence on one another.[34]

Fear of fearlessness

Thus one who has heard but does not examine
The doctrine which destroys all suffering,
And fears the fearless state
Trembles due to ignorance.

That all these will not exist in nirvāṇa
Does not frighten you [a Hīnayānist],
Why does their non-existence
Explained here cause you fright?[35]

Once we have been introduced to this doctrine of definite goodness, we can do one of two things: we can reflect upon it, engage with it and consider how to apply it, or we can forget it or ignore it. According to Nāgārjuna we adopt this second course out of fear. So another paradox rears its head: we fear being fearless. Fear being always on account of the ego, one result of seeing through the ego is that we become fearless. However, the 'I' that must do the seeing is also the 'I' that must be seen through. We necessarily fear this 'demise' of our delusion. Who will guarantee our safety if we are fearless? The confusion here arises out of our inability to imagine being without the 'I' and therefore without fear. When we try to imagine the 'I' itself being fearless, this seems impossible. We imagine that not wanting to look around for security, for things to rely on, will make us feel insecure. We even fear being free of suffering. We are comfortable with our fear and misery, and we would feel very unsure of our ground without them.

We may think we are meditating in order to gain Insight here and now, but is this really what we want?

We fear fearlessness in the same way that we fear non-violence. To act non-violently certainly appears to make one more vulnerable. You are dropping your defences, leaving yourself more open, more exposed. However, this very vulnerability can be disarming, and even when it doesn't succeed in disarming aggression, the lack of desire for retaliation and security renders you much less vulnerable at a mental and emotional level. You do not feed the escalating verbal aggression out of which most physical violence issues. At its most developed, non-violence is equivalent to non-ego; there is no fixed identification with the threatened self, and therefore no fear for it, and no violence in defence of it.

For Nāgārjuna, fear of fearlessness provides the material for a polemical dig at the Buddhist opponents of the Madhyamaka doctrine. Beneath their rejection Nāgārjuna detects a deep unease with the Dharma, an unconscious terror of what they themselves teach. The traditional teaching is that on the attainment of Enlightenment, there is no further rebirth – that is, that when the Enlightened individual dies, the *skandhas* that were the basis of his existence will not come together again. The follower of the Hīnayāna is obviously going to be happy with the idea that in the state of *nirvāṇa* there should be no *skandhas*. Nāgārjuna is suggesting, however, that the Hīnayāna position is inconsistent. If the Hīnayānist is inspired by the consideration that 'all these' aggregates will not exist in *nirvāṇa*, why should he be so alarmed by their non-existence now? Neither the ego nor the five *skandhas* have ever existed as absolutely real entities, and the attainment of Enlightenment is the point at which one fully realizes that truth. If, therefore, a follower of the Hīnayāna is happy to think that the five *skandhas* have no existence in the state of *nirvāṇa*, he should be equally happy to realize that they do not really exist here and now. If he is not prepared to countenance this corollary, he cannot really be taking his own teaching seriously.

This is not just ancient academic hair-splitting. Modern Buddhists who happily contemplate the future dissolution of the ego would probably change their tune were the dissolution of their ego to be about to happen right now. St Augustine's famous prayer, 'Oh Lord, make me chaste, but not yet', is a rueful insight into the inner conflict of the spiritual life. There is a parallel Buddhist story of an old lady who comes to her local temple every day to pray to the Buddha. 'Come and take me to *nirvāṇa*, away from this sorrowful existence' is her fervent and regular plea to the temple's huge Buddha figure. One day the priest at this temple decides to teach her a lesson. He creeps behind the statue of the Buddha while she is on her knees before it, begging to be released from the sufferings of *saṃsāra*, and he booms out, 'Your prayers are answered. I am coming for you – now!' With this unearthly response still echoing round the walls of the shrine, she is on her feet and running for the door, crying out 'Won't the Buddha let me have my little joke?'

This is very often the attitude with which we approach our practice of the Dharma. We may think we are meditating in order to gain insight here and now, but is this really what we want? Do we not rather want to have a few more good rebirths? Enlightenment is after all a kind of death – the end of everything we rely on and identify with. And how ready are we even for death in the ordinary sense? Having read the *Tibetan Book of the Dead*, or studied the lives of the great Buddhist renunciants like Milarepa, we might claim, 'I'm quite ready to die at any time,' but once death starts actually looming over us it is a different story. 'Any time' in the next thirty or fifty years feels rather different from 'any time' in the next week, say.

But if we do not want to go now, then essentially we do not want to go at all. If we really wanted Enlightenment in the future, we would really want it now. And if we are not interested in Enlightenment at the moment, how can we hold to the wish for Enlightenment in the future? We cannot really be genuinely happy with the idea of gaining Enlightenment after, say, ten million rebirths, but not with the idea of gaining it right now, if such a thing were possible. It is not, after all, that the ego will become non-existent at some future date. Nāgārjuna's whole argument here is that the ego is non-existent at this very moment.

All this is not to suggest that Enlightenment might be sprung on us before we are ready for it. Indeed, it is the preparation, the getting yourself ready, that sets up the momentum that will carry you, eventually, to the goal. But we do need to be clear what 'goal' means. It is not in some other place that the nature of reality becomes apparent; if we could only realize the fact, it is already manifesting here and now.

The non-definition of Nirvāṇa

'In liberation there is no self and are no aggregates.'
If liberation is asserted thus,
Why is the removal here of the self
And of the aggregates not liked by you?

If nirvāṇa is not a non-thing,
Just how could it have thingness?
The extinction of the misconception
Of things and non-things is called nirvāṇa.[36]

We may see in our mind's eye a vanishing point that we may call *nirvāṇa*, but this is only to say that we have reached the limits of the conditioned mind.

Nāgārjuna evidently feels the need, based upon the thinking current in his time, to address this issue in terms of things rather than processes, and thus characterize *nirvāṇa* in essentially negative terms as the extinction of the misconception of things and non-things. A more positive way of putting this would be to say that liberation consists in seeing processes rather than things. Nāgārjuna's language of 'non-things' and 'thing-ness' is a little cryptic, to say the least. This is because the answer to the question he poses is not available to the conditioned mind. It is the conditioned mind that asks questions, but it is also the conditioned mind that finds certain answers unintelligible, and the same conditioned mind that finds this rather frustrating.

In the Unconditioned mind, however, this frustration with the lack of an answer is simply not there. The answer is no longer necessary, as the question itself is no longer there. In the state of mind in which you ask the question, you cannot get a meaningful answer, while in the state of mind in which you can get the answer, you cannot meaningfully ask the question.

Throughout the Mahāyāna teachings we find an idea of *nirvāṇa* that is not any sort of thing or space or state of being, or any kind of personal existence. It is not subject to any kind of limitation or definition whatsoever. It is not even defined as being opposed to *saṃsāra*. It is called the *apratiṣṭhita nirvāṇa*, the 'non-established' or 'unlocalized' *nirvāṇa*. It is not established outside *saṃsāra*. It does not exist here as distinct from there. It is the *nirvāṇa* of no fixed point. Nāgārjuna speaks here of *nirvāṇa* as the extinction of misconceptions of *nirvāṇa* as being either a thing or not a thing. But the fact that it is not nothing does not mean that it is any kind of thing. He is saying, in other words, that while we can talk about *nirvāṇa*, we cannot do so in any way that really limits or defines it. At the same time it is also the extinction of the misconception of *nirvāṇa* as being either limited or unlimited. That it is not unlimited does not mean that it is limited.

If we think of *nirvāṇa* as a fixed point, however subtle or sublime, to which we may attain and of which we may take possession, we are really thinking of it as a glorified ego state. *Nirvāṇa* is not a sort of spiritual retirement home far from the madding crowd of suffering humanity, where we can settle down to enjoy our well-earned pension. *Nirvāṇa* is not a destination at which we arrive: it is the life of Enlightenment. It is a way of living, a process of perfectibility to which you can see no end. *Nirvāṇa* is the way you live, the way you have your being, when you have gone beyond the limitations of conditioned consciousness.

It is probably unwise to say that *nirvāṇa* is not a terminus, but we can certainly say that while it may be an end, we cannot see that end. All we can imagine from our standpoint is the process of growth and development stretching before us, one vista giving way to another, unendingly. What we see perhaps is a kind of vanishing point created by our fixed and limited perspective or vision, whereas in reality the lines apparently converging at a point upon the horizon remain parallel. We may see in our mind's eye a vanishing point that we call *nirvāṇa*, but this is only to say that we have reached the limits of the conditioned mind. That end point for the conditioned mind is where *nirvāṇa* no doubt begins a yet further process of growth and development. The *White Lotus Sūtra* offers an image for this necessarily limited vision of the goal. In it, the Buddha speaks of a magic city which he has conjured up in order to encourage weary travellers to continue their journey. But when they get there, they find that it is no more than a halfway house.[37] Similarly, beyond our ordinary conception of *nirvāṇa* there are higher, broader, deeper *nirvāṇas*, to which we have no conceptual access at all.

Nāgārjuna's emphasis on the practices productive of high status, such as generosity and moral living, reflects the spiritual principle that any goal becomes a new starting point. Nāgārjuna's intention is that the king should commit himself to such practices so as to achieve high status, peace of mind, happiness and further success, as well as develop the higher practices that will carry him towards definite goodness. To put it another way, *nirvāṇa* is a process just as *saṃsāra* is a process. The process of conditioned co-production (*pratītya-samutpāda*) that characterizes *saṃsāra* also characterizes *nirvāṇa*, although it works in a different way. If *saṃsāra* is thought of as a cyclical process, then *nirvāṇa* may be imagined as a kind of spiral. According to the teaching of the *nidānas* there are twelve links or *nidānas* making up the cycle of *saṃsāra*, which may be summarized as follows: our present rebirth arises in dependence on ignorance; craving arises in dependence on sense contact and the feeling associated with that contact, and grasping on the basis of craving, leading to death and another rebirth. But there are also twelve positive *nidānas* making up a spiral path leading from an awareness of the suffering (*duḥkha*) bound up with the cycle of *saṃsāra*. Faith arises in dependence on suffering; joy in dependence on faith, and after that rapture, and then bliss and concentration; knowledge and vision of things as they really are arises on the basis of concentration, and the series culminates with knowledge of the destruction of the *āśravas* or 'cankers' (craving for sense pleasures, craving for existence, and ignorance).[38]

This is the creative mind taken to its highest degree of development. But it does not mark an end to the spiral process. It is a jumping-off point for further development, the last visible stage of a process that continues indefinitely. *Nirvāṇa* is a term used to indicate the unlimited nature of the process of growth and development, a final term to designate the fact that there can be no end to that positive process, no final turn of the spiral. Enlightenment is a life, but not in the sense that it goes on and on in time; it is a living process that continues beyond time, indeed, beyond the very distinction between time and timelessness.

Emptiness as a mirage

A form seen from a distance
Is seen clearly by those nearby.
If a mirage were water, why
Is water not seen by those nearby?

The way this world is seen
As real by those afar,
Is not so seen by those nearby
[For whom it is] signless like a mirage.

Just as a mirage is like water but is
Not water and does not in fact exist [as water],
So the aggregates are like a self but are
Not selves and do not in fact exist [as selves].[39]

The simile of the mirage is a popular one in Indian thought, and especially in Mahāyāna Buddhism. If you see something

> The spiritually immature, who do not examine their experience of the world closely enough to see it as it really is, see a world of substantial things, peopled by fixed selves.

from a distance, you do not see it very clearly. If someone is standing nearer than you are to whatever you are looking at, they will usually be able to see it much more clearly than you can. In the case of the mirage, however, which is an optical illusion – most commonly of water in the desert – the opposite is true. From a distance, you see what seems to be water, but as you approach it you find that there is no water there but only desert. This is the nature of a mirage: what you see from a distance you do not see when you come closer. If you think that the water you see will quench your thirst, you will inevitably be disappointed when you get nearer and find that there is only desert.

The spiritually immature, who do not examine their experience of the world closely enough to see it as it really is, see a world of substantial things, peopled by fixed selves. The spiritually mature, who reflect on their experience mindfully and dispassionately, realize that there is really nothing substantial, nothing fixed there at all. There is no water in the desert. If you really look closely at your experience, without losing sight of it in emotional reactions to it, you will see that it is not real in quite the way you took it to be; it is only provisionally, relatively real. This idea is one to which we have, unsurprisingly, a deep resistance. The arising of true Insight, when we see things as they really are, has therefore to occur at a very deep level. However, when such Insight does arise, the qualities that the things around us seemed to possess when our vision was distorted by craving, aversion or indifference fade away like a mirage when we come closer and see them as they really are. The poet Thomas Campbell observed that ''tis distance lends enchantment to the view', and this is certainly our situation in the world. We are enchanted by a mirage that promises to quench our 'thirst' for something permanent, substantial, and satisfying, but which never does so.

Just as the *skandhas* or aggregates seem to add up to something that is actually there, in the form of a substantial fixed self, so the mirage really appears to be water. We certainly do see something, but what we see is not really water. Similarly, the aggregates are there, but they do not amount to or include the ego-self that we read into them. What we see from a distance, so to speak, is the ego-self. But when we look more closely all we find are the *skandhas*, and when we go closer still and investigate each *skandha* individually, we find that they too do not exist as distinct, independent entities.

In the following verse, Nāgārjuna qualifies this to rule out any possibility of misinterpreting his teaching as simple nihilism.

Having thought a mirage to be
Water and then having gone there,
He would just be stupid to surmise
'That water does not exist.'[40]

The mere fact that one is able to mistake the mirage for water means that there is indeed something for which the mirage can be mistaken. Water does exist; it just doesn't exist where you think it does when you are taken in by the mirage. Similarly, although the self does not in fact possess the qualities of permanence and changelessness, which we wrongly attribute to it, those qualities do exist elsewhere. If you did not find the qualities of the Unconditioned in conditioned things, such as the self and its objects, you would be foolish to conclude from this that those qualities did not exist at all. Discovering that there is no water to be found in the mirage, you would be foolish to conclude that there is no such thing as water anywhere. Yet this is exactly what we do when we look in the wrong place for happiness, security, permanence, truth, or beauty. Having exhausted the possibilities for satisfaction in our quest to find these qualities where we expect to find them, we assume that they are not to be found anywhere. In fact, they are available to us here and now, but only if we change the whole direction of our life. This means abandoning habits of mind so deeply ingrained that we can barely envisage any other way of being. It means abandoning the search for happiness altogether, and instead following the path of ethical action from which happiness arises as an unintended, albeit very welcome, by-product.

> *If through knowing what is correct and true*
> *He does not assert existence and non-existence*
> *And thereby [you think] he believes in non-existence,*
> *Why should he not be a follower of existence?*
>
> *If from refuting [inherent] existence*
> *Non-existence then accrues to him,*
> *Why from refuting non-existence*
> *Would existence not accrue to him?*
>
> *Those who rely on enlightenment*
> *Have no nihilistic thesis,*
> *Behaviour or thought, how can*
> *They be seen as nihilists?*[41]

As a follower of the Madhyamaka tradition, Nāgārjuna asserts neither existence nor non-existence, neither eternalism nor nihilism. However, with its talk of the void and the extinction of the ego, the Śūnyavāda, or 'way of emptiness' (another name for the Madhyamaka), can quite pardonably be mistaken for a nihilistic philosophy. And in Nāgārjuna's time other Buddhists, presumably followers of the Hīnayāna, did regard it in this way. In response to this misunderstanding, Nāgārjuna points out that the Śūnyavāda refutes both eternalism and nihilism. If he comes to be accused of being a nihilist because he refutes the inherent existence of things, then he could also be accused of the opposite. After all, he also refutes the nihilistic view that things do not exist at all. Why not accuse him, then, of being an eternalist? In other words, he is trying to show that the Hīnayānist objections are self-contradictory.

The next point Nāgārjuna makes is that followers of the Śūnyavāda have as their declared aim *samyaksambodhi*, complete and perfect Enlightenment. How, with this goal in view, can their doctrine, ethics or thinking be nihilistic? It is, after all, the same *bodhi* as that to which their critics aspire – not a state of non-existence. In order to arrive at this same goal, they both must follow essentially the same ethical code, essentially the same practices of meditation, and essentially the same teachings about Enlightenment.

Chapter Four

....

Nothing left at all?

Ask the worldly ones, the Sāṃkhyas,
Owl-Followers and Nirgranthas,
The proponents of a person and aggregates,
If they propound what passes beyond 'is' and 'is not'.[42]

Here, Nāgārjuna throws down a challenge to various non-Buddhist schools. The 'worldly ones', Lokāyatikas, are of course the materialists.[43] The Sāṃkhyas make an absolute distinction between the material world (*prakṛti*) and the spiritual world (*puruṣa*) and they uphold a philosophy of causation called *satkāryavāda*, the view that cause and effect are identical. The Owl-followers are the Vaiśeṣikas, or pluralists, who attempt to analyze experience into its ultimate elements.[44] The Nirgranthas are the Jains, whose tradition was founded by a near-contemporary of the Buddha called Mahāvīra.[45] In one way or another, all these spiritual traditions uphold a belief in the absolute reality of the person and the aggregates. So Nāgārjuna issues his challenge. Ask them, he

For someone who has no real spiritual experience, whose whole life is bound up with knowledge as mediated by concepts, this is indeed a teaching of non-existence or nihilism.

says, if they have a teaching that goes beyond all concepts whatsoever, a teaching that sees through the dualism of existence and non-existence.

The Śūnyavāda is nihilistic to those whose reality is wholly mundane. It seems nihilistic only if what it negates is seen as everything. To paraphrase a passage towards the end of *The World as Will and Idea*, Schopenhauer in effect observes that to one to whom the world 'with all its suns and galaxies' is everything, *nirvāṇa* is nothing. If you were to speak to the man in the street about the inherent meaninglessness of worldly life, and were to suggest to him that there could be a way of life in which there was no job, no marriage, no family, no football, he would say that this would leave him with nothing. For him, life without a job and so on is no life at all. Or if you see sex, or having fun, or making money, or even the arts, as everything, then the Dharma, when it suggests that these things are of no real importance in the larger scheme of things, can appear nihilistic. Thus Buddhism generally can be seen as nihilistic from the worldly point of view.

Critics of the Śūnyavāda doctrine may renounce mundane life in favour of the spiritual life, but ultimately they remain mired in the mundane world so long as they take their renunciation as having some kind of absolute validity, so long as they get caught up in the idea of the spiritual life and identify with it absolutely. If, for you, conceptualized reality is everything, when concepts are repudiated, nothing is left. And the Śūnyavāda does just this: it repudiates all concepts. For someone who has no real spiritual experience, whose whole life is bound up with knowledge as mediated by concepts, this is indeed a teaching of non-existence or nihilism.

Renunciation is not an absolute value. You give up what is relatively satisfying in order to attain something that is truly satisfying. The idea is not to throw away the good that you find in the things you enjoy, but to imagine that good refined and heightened to an infinite degree. If, for example, you obtain great satisfaction from your family, and for you family life is everything, you certainly won't want to give that up. The

Buddhist invitation is simply to imagine a much wider family, what you might call the 'spiritual family', a circle of spiritual friendship that is as loyal and selfless as any parent should be towards their offspring. This is the ideal of the Sangha. Of course, the reality is that the Sangha is rarely quite as generous and kind and forgiving as it ideally should be, but that is what ideals are for – to give us something to aim towards.

There is no profit in shielding ourselves from the truth of things, which is that worldly pleasures and attachments are unsure and impermanent. Nor can we duck the challenges that this truth gives us. Sooner or later we have to confront the demands of the spiritual life, which may not be at all easy. But when we do so our purpose will be to grow and develop. We have to put aside certain activities and values that we have perhaps held dear in the past, in order to realize greater things.

The self is negated with similar provisos. If you fully identify with the ego-self, there is little to be gained from renouncing it unless at the same time you can see the possibility of transcending it. It should be questioned and broken down only in order to reveal a sense of identity that is infinitely more refined. It is put in its proper place as a lower self in order that you may realize what you are in a much higher sense.

Giving things up need not involve hardship, so long as you remain in good contact with your spiritual friends. If, for example, you are married, you need to seek out other married members of the Sangha and find out how they manage to be fully committed to the spiritual life while fulfilling their responsibilities as husbands and wives, fathers and mothers. Likewise, if you are attracted to the life of a homeless and celibate wanderer, you can go to people who are already living in that way and talk to them about how they took up that lifestyle in the first place and how they live it on a daily basis.

It is not a question of some theoretical principle that you must follow in order to be a good Buddhist. It is about transforming your life in a way that does justice to what you are and what you wish to be. If you are not sure that some course of action is feasible, check it out with others who have followed it successfully. This is one of the very great benefits of the Sangha. Here are other people, not very different from yourself, who are actually involved in the kind of life that you are thinking of leading. The teachings of Śūnyavāda, of the *Diamond Sūtra*, or of the Zen masters, mean very little without the community of committed followers who know from their own experience how to put those teachings into practice.

> *Thereby know that the ambrosia*
> *Of the Buddhas' teaching is called profound,*
> *An uncommon doctrine passing*
> *Far beyond existence and non-existence.*[46]

It is because the Buddha's teaching goes beyond ideas of existence and non-existence, beyond all concepts, that it is called profound. It is called ambrosia or nectar (*amṛta*) in order to suggest the complete suffusion of the experience of emptiness with the profound bliss that comes with the extinction of suffering.

What is this world?

> *Ultimately how could the world exist with a nature*
> *Which has gone beyond the past, the present*
> *And the future, not going when destroyed,*
> *Not coming and not staying even for an instant?*
>
> *Because in reality there is*
> *No coming, going or staying,*
> *What ultimate difference is there*
> *Then between the world and nirvāṇa?*
>
> *If there is no staying, there can be*
> *No production and no cessation.*
> *Then how could production, staying and*
> *Cessation ultimately exist?*[47]

In this rather obscure passage Nāgārjuna asks how if, in the ultimate sense, there can be no past, present or future, the world itself can exist as perceived in those terms. We perceive the world in terms of time, of its being a process of arising, continuing and stopping. But in reality there is no coming or going or remaining, no production, cessation or staying. Each process exists only in a relative sense, in relation to its opposite. Not that the world is ultimately unreal. What we read into the world is unreal, including the distinction between real and unreal. *Saṃsāra* and *nirvāṇa* are not eternally distinct realities. The distinction between them comes from our dualistic way of thinking, our delusion that we can categorize the world and what is beyond the world, separate *saṃsāra* and *nirvāṇa* in any way other than as a practical expedient.

> You can overcome dualism only by initially adopting a dualistic position. As the Tantrics were to say later on, you have to get rid of dirt with dirt.

Nāgārjuna is not putting forward this proposition to win assent on a conceptual level. He is not asserting a philosophy, not teaching a monism. His intention is the practical one of clearing away the dualistic views that obscure the path to Enlightenment. The point is that we cannot help but think dualistically, even while we are engaged in uprooting dualistic concepts. As soon as you envisage a distinction between being dualistic and being non-dualistic, you are being dualistic. But you have to do this in order to have any chance of breaking down your dualistic vision.

It is the paradox of the goose in the bottle. Even though you cannot get the goose out of the bottle without either breaking the bottle or injuring the goose, that is what you have to do. You can overcome dualism only by initially adopting a dualistic standpoint. As the Tantrics were to say later on, you have to get rid of dirt with dirt. It is like the traditional Indian way of washing clothes. You take mud from the river and use it like soap, rubbing it into the clothes and then rinsing them out. In this way you use dirt to get rid of dirt.[48] Or it is like sailing against the wind by tacking this way and that. You use the wind that is blowing against you to make progress against the wind. Likewise, you get rid of concepts with concepts, dualism by means of dualism.

What is this moment?

How are things non-momentary
If they are always changing?
If they do not change, then how
In fact can they be altered?

Do they become momentary through
Partial or complete disintegration?
Because an inequality is not apprehended,
This momentariness cannot be admitted.

When a thing ceases to exist through momentariness,
How can anything be old?
When a thing is non-momentary due to constancy
How can anything be old?

Since a moment ends it must have
A beginning and a middle,
This triple nature of a moment means
That the world never abides for an instant.

Also the beginning, middle and end
Are to be analyzed like a moment;
Therefore, beginning, middle and end
Are not [produced] from self or other.[49]

A school of Buddhist thought in Nāgārjuna's time held that nothing lasted for more than a split second, and that what seemed to be things were just a sequence of dharmas popping up – each for a split second – and then disappearing.

54

If these dharmas were very similar, they created an illusion of a single thing, like the way a film-reel creates the illusion of continuity out of a succession of separate images or frames. It is this philosophy of

The world itself does not exist 'momentarily' even for a moment.

momentariness (*kṣaṇikavāda*) that Nāgārjuna has in his sights in these verses. The main problem with it is that it attempts to explain flow, continuity, process, change, or coming and going, by discontinuity, by positing a succession of discrete entities, which is contradictory. Nāgārjuna points out that if one of these moments, however tiny, appears and disappears, then logically it must have a beginning, a middle, and an end. That is, it is divisible into these three elements at the very least. Therefore, no moment can be said to be absolutely irreducible. Anything you decide to call a moment must consist of further moments, themselves infinitely divisible in their turn. There is, in fact, nothing that exists momentarily at all. The world itself does not exist 'momentarily' even for a moment.

What is this object?

Due to having many parts 'one' does not exist,
There is not anything which is without parts,
Further without 'one' 'many' does not exist
And without existence there is no non-existence.[50]

The Abhidharma's analysis of the world of our experience into dharmas, conceived as the ultimate components of existence, gets the same treatment as the philosophy of momentariness.[51] What Nāgārjuna has done with respect to time, he now does with regard to space.

Whole philosophical schools are built upon this fundamental error. They invest a concept with ultimate reality, when in fact it owes its 'existence' to what it is not.

55

Anything conceived as a separable entity must logically be subject to further analysis. There is nothing that cannot be subdivided into parts, so nothing you can call 'one' can have any inherent existence. You can never get down to something that can be characterized simply as 'one'. As soon as you have 'one' you also have 'many'. Similarly, every part is itself a whole that can be analyzed into further parts. Whether it is the one and the many, or the whole and its parts, the terms are co-relative. One cannot therefore regard the parts as real and the whole as unreal, which is what the Abhidharma does, any more than one can regard the whole as real and the parts as essentially unreal, which is more like the conventional way people see things.

Again Nāgārjuna is examining the way we lose sight of the reality of any concept, and the truth behind any kind of distinction. This truth is that whatever that concept may be, it is dependent upon its opposite, upon whatever it is distinct from. Whole philosophical schools are built upon this fundamental error. They invest a concept with ultimate reality, when in fact it owes its 'existence' to what it is not.

The end of the world

If through destruction or an antidote
An existent ceases to exist,
How could there be destruction or
An antidote without an existent?

Ultimately the world cannot
Through nirvāṇa disappear.
Asked whether it had an end
The Conqueror was silent.[52]

The idea of a poison and its antidote is another case of interdependent duality; the antidote exists only in relation to the poison. Thus *nirvāṇa*, as the antidote to the sufferings of conditioned existence, exists only in relation to those sufferings, to *saṃsāra*. For *nirvāṇa* to be there, suffering has to be there as well. So long as you hold on to the idea of an end to suffering, there can be no end to suffering. You cannot have one without the other. The path that leads away from suffering exists only in relation to its point of

The real freedom is where there is no world and no freedom from the world.

departure, which is suffering itself. Hence you can never arrive at *nirvāṇa*, at least as conceived in terms of the antidote to the suffering of *saṃsāra*. *Nirvāṇa* as the cessation of suffering is like getting out of prison and leaving the prison still there behind you. Real freedom is where there is no prison at all, and even, we might say, where there is no freedom either: no prison and therefore no freedom from prison. In the same way, freedom from the world is not real freedom. The real freedom is where there is no world and no freedom from the world.

Abstruse as this idea may sound, it can be applied even at a quite ordinary level of spiritual practice. If when you meditate you are simply concerned to get away from a certain aspect of your experience, you will not get very far. Mindfulness is the practice of being present with the whole of your experience, bad as well as good, painful as well as pleasant. Even negative states of mind must at some point be *transformed*, not just pushed away.

The ground beneath our feet

Because he did not teach this profound doctrine
To worldly beings who were not receptacles,
The all-knowing one is therefore known
As omniscient by the wise.

Thus the doctrine of definite goodness
Was taught by the perfect Buddhas
The seers of reality, as profound,
Unapprehendable and baseless.[53]

In his opening paean to the Buddha, Nāgārjuna acknowledges him as 'all-knowing'. He now tells us in what way the Buddha is omniscient, since this omniscience is not what we usually understand by the term. It consists, he tells us, simply in knowing whom to teach and what to teach them. It is not so much a question of the amount of the information, but of its relevance. It is a knowledge that is unapprehendable in that it is not to be understood in dualistic terms. It is baseless, firstly in that it does not depend on anything else. It is not an amassing of facts that might be learned from someone; it comes from within. Secondly, it is baseless in that the Buddha's teaching does not provide a platform for false views.

Frightened by this baseless doctrine,
Delighting in a base, not passing
Beyond existence and non-existence,
Unintelligent beings ruin themselves.[54]

If we do not feel the ground beneath our feet, how can we experience it as it really is? How can we experience existence as baseless unless we can first rest our weight fully on that base?

The adjective 'baseless' used in conjunction with the noun 'doctrine' might seem to suggest, pejoratively, that the doctrine is unreliable and untrue. However, in this context it means that the content or meaning of the doctrine is baseless in the sense that it is not to be settled down in, or rested upon, or relied on for security, or taken as having absolute validity.

If we truly get a sense of transcendental wisdom, we are frightened by it, because it teaches that there is nothing for us to settle down in, nothing in the world that is ultimately real. Yet our lives are dedicated to seeking fulfilment by stemming the flow of experience, by setting up false ideas of things, of self and other. We try to turn the impermanent into something permanent. We approach a situation that is in reality free and fluid and deal with it as if it was fixed, settled, 'a base'. We need it to be settled so that we can settle down in it. We delight in a base in the sense of feeling secure in our dependence upon impermanent 'things', our grasping after existence or non-existence. If we do nothing to get beyond this reliance upon concepts, we are without a firm footing in reality, and so we ruin and waste our life.

Much of the time, even, we do not properly *delight* in a base. We do not really relish where we are, yet it does not occur to us to look further. We may want to move from a small house to a bigger house, or exchange a small car for a bigger car, but we don't think of moving from houses and cars and so on as our base to a more spiritual base. In our fear of the unknown, we prefer to hang on discontentedly to the base we have rather than trying to move towards a better one.

If we are not in fact able to delight in a base, and do not feel frightened by this 'baseless doctrine', it may be that we are not ready for such a doctrine. We have to start from where we are, which may mean starting from an apparently secure but in reality unreliable base. We may be locked into a negative view of things and be unable to commit ourselves to anything. In order to transcend any kind of a base, we need a positive and provisionally secure base from which to begin. If we do not feel the ground beneath our feet, how can we experience it as it really is? How can we experience existence as baseless unless we can first rest our weight fully on that base?

The Sangha is meant to provide an emotionally positive, open-ended base, allowing us room to grow and develop, and ideally encouraging us always to move beyond whatever base we make of it. It will even provide a base in which we may take a quite healthy delight. There can be nothing wrong with enjoying the things around us, so long as what we delight in leads us on to other interests, other 'bases' that are more refined, more subtle and more ethical. Following such a path, the 'base' in which you delight eventually drops away altogether. All we have to do is keep letting go of what we think we know; we have to avoid settling down in any sense of being sure of ourselves, of being secure in the absolute validity of our perspective.

Being able to settle down in a way that is committed but at the same time provisional is very much a matter of integration. It is a matter of bringing your emotions and desires into harmony with your ideals and highest aspirations, so that you are no longer thrown hither and thither by your whims and fancies. At the same time, you are aware that however rewarding or enjoyable a situation may be, it is neither permanent nor ultimately fulfilling. You will not, therefore, become so settled in it that you lose sight of your higher aspirations. You enjoy the meditation group, the Buddhist movement, the centre or community, the retreat facility, the right livelihood business, only to the extent that these situations enable you to grow and develop. But if need be, you are ready to move on. You do not 'delight in a base' in the sense of getting entrenched in your situation, expecting other members of the group or community to reinforce your little habits and settled ways. You will not resent new people with new ideas, nor will you assume that this is where you will continue indefinitely.

It is important not to apply Nāgārjuna's warning here too literally. A necessary condition of ascending a flight of steps is that you will for an instant rest on each step in turn. Even this image is not to be taken too literally, if it suggests an attitude of skipping lightly from one step to the next. Setting no great store by anything, and feeling no human attachment or responsibility at all, is nihilism, not spiritual maturity. The mind that is not driven by its attachments is one thing; the butterfly mind is quite another.

In his teaching of high status and definite goodness, Nāgārjuna seems to be saying that although we should avoid gathering useless things, we still need to gather things of relative value. Whatever they are, however, they should be appreciated as things that cannot be relied on in an absolute sense. We need to see that any situation is conditioned and impermanent, and that we may need to move on from it at some point if we are to grow.

O King, lest you be ruined
I will explain through the scriptures
The mode of the supramundane,
The reality that relies not on dualism.

This profundity which liberates
And is beyond both sin and virtue
Has not been tasted by those who fear the baseless,
The others, the Forders and even by ourselves.[55]

'The Forders' are the leaders of various non-Buddhist philosophical schools, and 'ourselves' may refer to those Buddhists, such as the followers of the Hīnayāna, who do not accept the Madhyamaka viewpoint. In a more profound sense, it can be taken to refer to the inherent ungraspableness of any doctrinal presentation of reality. There is in reality no-one who tastes, nor any doctrine to be tasted. The doctrine of emptiness is not tasted by those who do not accept it; nor is it tasted even by those who accept it in all its profundity.

> The doctrine of emptiness is not tasted by those who do not accept it; nor is it tasted even by those who accept it in all its profundity.

Chapter Five

Elements and arguments

Convincing us to doubt

A person is not earth, not water,
Not fire, not wind, not space,
Not consciousness and not all of them;
What person is there other than these?

Just as the person is not an ultimate
But a composite of six constituents,
So each of them in turn is a
Composite and not an ultimate.

The aggregates are not the self, they are not in it,
It is not in them, without them it is not,
It is not mixed with the aggregates like fire and fuel,
Therefore how can the self exist?

The three elements are not earth, they are not in it,
It is not in them, without them it is not;
Since this applies to each,
They like the self are false.

By themselves earth, water, fire and wind
Do not inherently exist;
When any three are absent, there cannot be one,
When one is absent, so too are the three.

If when three are absent, the one does not exist
And if when one is absent, the three do not exist,
Then each itself does not exist;
How can they produce a composite?

Otherwise if each itself exists,
Why without fuel is there no fire?
Likewise why is there no water, wind or earth
Without motility, hardness or cohesion?

If [it is answered that] fire is well known [not to exist
Without fuel but the other three elements exist
Independently], how could your three exist in themselves
Without the others? It is impossible for the three
Not to accord with dependent-arising.

How can those existing by themselves
Be mutually dependent?
How can those which exist not by themselves
Be mutually dependent?

If as individuals they do not exist,
But where there is one, the other three are there,
Then if unmixed, they are not in one place,
And if mixed, they cease to be individuals.

The elements do not themselves exist individually,
So how could their own individual characters do so?
What do not themselves individually exist cannot
    predominate;
Their characters are regarded as conventionalities.

This mode of refutation is also to be applied
To colours, odours, tastes and objects of touch,
Eye, consciousness and form,
Ignorance, action and birth,

Agent, object, acting and number,
Possession, cause, effect and time,
Short and long and so forth,
Name and name-bearer as well.[56]

Whether people are really converted by such close reasoning, or really change the way they experience their life because of it, is perhaps questionable, especially today. Our experience shows us that the self does exist, at least in certain quite

Just because you have lost an argument does not mean that your position is necessarily wrong.

definite respects, and we seem to be able to accept the evident absence of the self within the elements as a puzzle, a living contradiction, perhaps in the same way that we accept the paradoxes of modern science. However, the ancient Indians had what seems to have been a misplaced trust in the power of logical reasoning – either that or they responded to hard logical argument in a way that people these days do not. We tend to be suspicious of any argument that is made too watertight. It can seem rather too clever to be convincing, signalling desperation and doubt more than confidence. Who is he really trying to convince, we ask ourselves, me or himself? If we are not motivated by simple, straightforward arguments, is complicating them the solution? Nāgārjuna would certainly seem to believe so, as his argument here becomes rather more sophisticated than seems strictly useful.

For whatever reason, the thoroughly worked, not to say overworked, logical argument seems to have been necessary to appeal to the ancient Indian mind. In Nāgārjuna's time, great public debates involving famous rival teachers were common in India. The defeated teacher would have to become the disciple of his vanquisher, taking all his disciples with him. This was how seriously public debate was taken in those days. Today, people might wonder what all the fuss was about. Just because you have lost an argument does not mean that your position is necessarily wrong. It may just mean that your opponent is more skilled at argument than you are, not that he has the truth on his side. Why make such a big change to your life simply because you have been defeated in a debate?

But this attitude persisted in India down the centuries. Śāntideva, a Madhyamaka teacher of a later period, certainly has it. In the *Bodhicaryāvatāra*, for example, he puts forward all sorts of ingenious reasons why we should not give way to anger, but their overall effect can be curiously irritating, and therefore self-defeating.[57] When his arguments become too relentlessly unanswerable you begin to distrust them. Yes, it is illogical to be angry, and yes, the ego is an illusion – as many neuroscientists and psychiatrists confirm today – but the question is not whether that can be accepted on a purely conceptual level, but whether the truth of the argument is experienced and absorbed emotionally.

Even in present-day Tibet we find that the Gelugpas, who follow the Madhyamaka tradition, have a cast-iron faith in the power of logic to convey the essential truth of the Dharma. Whereas Milarepa, the founder of the Kagyupa tradition, goes almost entirely by inspiration and personal experience, Je Tsongkhapa, the great Gelugpa teacher, follows the guidance of the scriptures and strict reasoning. Of course, Tsongkhapa brings his own experience to bear upon his understanding, but personal experience is not usually at the forefront of his teaching.

In Europe, too, the scholastic philosophers and theologians of the middle ages displayed a tremendous faith in the power of reason and logic. The ancient Greek world also leaves the impression of people relishing the use of reason, not only taking it seriously but being fascinated by it. And yet, like those of Nāgārjuna, the arguments of Socrates seem sometimes less than compelling, even sophistical. Maybe we do not need all that much logical proof of the nature of reality. The real proof of any pudding is in the eating. When we try to understand and interpret the ancient teachings of the Madhyamaka for ourselves, it is important to bear in mind their real purpose and relate the arguments to our own experience of life.

All the same, there is method in the exhaustive way Nāgārjuna hunts the rational mind out of its holes. To be brought up sharp against the limitations of one's ordinary consciousness is utterly frustrating, but nonetheless entirely necessary if one is to apprehend the truth of things. To imagine that you have arrived at that point when you have not even stretched your ordinary consciousness is a big mistake. It is by exhausting the possibilities of rational thought that we enable the truth of things to reveal itself. There is no use in giving up on the possibilities of penetrating reality with the dualistic mind prematurely. In fact, there should be no conscious decision to renounce the cutting edge of reason in our search for truth. Such a decision can only be another ploy by the conceptualizing mind to grasp at the truth, one that short-circuits the quest altogether. Only when one has truly arrived at the limits of one's thinking, one might say, can one become aware that the truth cannot be thought, that it can only, in the final instance, be experienced directly for what it is.

We may imagine that all this is too obvious to need reflecting upon, but it is our facile dismissal of the obvious that holds reality at bay.

First Nāgārjuna recaps some of the basics of his doctrine. A person is composite, and the constituents of that composite are themselves composite. A person is not to be identified with any one of the five aggregates or six elements, nor with a combination of all of them, nor with an existence apart from them. They are not in the self, nor is the self in them, and yet without them the self has no existence. Following this argument, you begin to get the idea of the self, of 'being' in the ultimate sense, as something self-contradictory, even absurd, to the extent that you begin to doubt your own existence.

The aggregates and the elements cannot be said either to exist or not to exist. Nāgārjuna shows, at length, that the elements depend upon one another for their existence, which means that they must exist, and at the same time he shows that they cannot exist in the sense of having an independent existence. If we think of things as embodying a varying mixture of the elements, and say simply that what we conventionally acknowledge as 'earth' is always a mixture of the elements in which earth predominates, then how can we identify 'earth' as an individual element at all? The same goes for the perceptual situation, in which eye, consciousness, and form all arise in dependence upon one another. Sense consciousness and external forms are two poles of a single process; they are not ultimately separate. Nor can we say even that ignorance is real in the sense of being ultimately separable from the karmic actions to which it gives rise and which eventually result in rebirth. We are a process in which we may identify elements like ignorance, skilful or unskilful actions and so on for practical purposes, but these elements have no independent reality.

The relationship between the things we distinguish in the world, especially between the self and those elements of its experience with which it identifies most closely, is thus shown to be impossible to pin down. The way the self is usually taken for granted as existing is shown to be quite literally baseless. Indeed, the self oughtn't to be there at all. The idea of a self in the ordinary sense is quite illogical, even self-contradictory. In other words, Nāgārjuna is trying to transform our experience of ourselves, trying to get us out of the habit of taking ourselves as seriously as we usually do, trying to stop us from settling down in ourselves as though we were something fixed and final. He wants to return us to what Walt Whitman calls 'the terrible doubt of appearances',[58] or what in the Zen tradition is often referred to as the 'Great Doubt'. He wants to shake our confidence in the reality of what we now experience as our 'self'.

Are we immediately shaken by the logical inconsistencies in our view of ourselves? Probably not. But we can reflect more closely upon that view. We can look out for the little manifestations in our daily life of the essential incoherence of our assumptions about that life. We can start by reflecting on what has brought us to where we are now. We can look back, for example, and see how we have changed over time. In so doing, we can be aware that further change is possible. We might reflect in this way: I am not the finished article; what I am now is not fixed and final. I am still on the assembly line. I am still in transition. What I am now I shall not be tomorrow. There may be growth in some areas, deterioration in others. How real, therefore, is the self with which I identify today?

Impermanence cannot be understood fully simply as a concept. We know perfectly well that things are impermanent, but in our heart of hearts we understand what this means and we are deeply afraid. Impermanence has to be experienced in ourselves and the world around us, moment by moment. We must also respect the power of this truth, and recognize how deeply we resist it. In the city, we see houses and office blocks coming down, and new ones going up. Shops close and new ones open. In the countryside, we see that the corn that was standing yesterday has today been harvested; only the straw remains, gathered in bales. Nature itself is a constant round of birth and death, bloom and fade, erosion and sedimentation, crack and slide. What we see today will not be there tomorrow. How real, therefore, is the world we see today? We may imagine that all this is too obvious to need reflecting upon, but it is our facile dismissal of the obvious that holds reality at bay.

Exchanging illusory water for real nectar

Earth, water, fire and wind,
Tall and short, subtle and coarse,
Virtue and so forth are said by the Subduer
To cease in the consciousness [of reality].

The spheres of earth, water, fire
And wind do not appear to that
Undemonstrable consciousness,
Complete lord over the limitless.

Here tall and short, subtle and coarse,
Virtue and non-virtue
And here names and forms
All cease to be.[59]

A net of concepts can in the
end catch only concepts.

These verses describe how the 'lord over the limitless' sees into reality itself. The Enlightened consciousness sees through conditioned existence. That is, it sees through the attempt by the conditioned consciousness to catch reality in the net of concepts or 'names', catching in that net both ideas of the self and what is not the self. However, Nāgārjuna's concern as always is to address the unenlightened mind's assumption that if reality is not to be found amongst its objects, it is to be found nowhere. If the 'things' we catch in our net of names prove to be empty of reality, if reality slips through that net, however finely woven it may be, this does not mean that reality is nothing. It means that a net of concepts can in the end catch only concepts.

What was not known is known
To consciousness as [the reality of] all
That appeared before. Thereby these phenomena
Later cease to be in consciousness.

All these phenomena related to beings
Are seen as fuel for the fire of consciousness,
They are consumed through being burned
By the light of true discrimination.[60]

The first of these two verses is especially cryptic, but it can be illustrated by going back to the analogy of the mirage in the desert. When you get near to the mirage, it is not that you see nothing at all, but that what you see is not the water you expected to find. Instead, you see what was really there all along. The appearance of the water ceases, and you see what was behind that illusion. The reality of things is missed because we see those things as 'things' rather than as unreal appearances. When the reality behind phenomena appears, those phenomena are seen through.

The reality is later ascertained
Of what was formerly imputed by ignorance;
When a thing is not found,
How can there be a non-thing?

Because the phenomena of forms are
Only names, space too is only a name;
Without the elements how could forms exist?
Therefore even 'name-only' does not exist.

Feelings, discriminations, factors of composition
And consciousnesses are to be considered
Like the elements and the self, thereby
The six constituents are selfless.[61]

'When a thing is not found, how can there be a non-thing?' This, too, can be understood in the light of the analogy of the mirage. What you falsely perceived to be water is later clearly seen to be desert. When that water is not found, nothing has been destroyed, nothing has been lost, since the water was never there in the first place. Similarly, in *nirvāṇa*, nothing is lost. It is not as though *saṃsāra* no longer exists, or has been destroyed, but rather that you have realized the true nature of *saṃsāra*. If the 'thing' was never there in the first place, you are not left with a lack of a thing. Even the idea of 'name-only' is itself just a name, an idea. Emptiness itself is empty. When *nirvāṇa* is described as 'void' it is only natural for people to imagine it in terms of what it will not be – no wives or husbands, no children, no job, no pleasures and enjoyments, no world. But in fact, *nirvāṇa* is a state not of deprivation, but of fulfilment. It is not that you lose things, but that you have the reality of things.

Let us further consider this analogy of the mirage of water in a way that brings us a little closer to how Enlightenment positively changes our experience. When we look at the mirage, we think we can see water, and of course that is probably what we want – so we go towards it looking forward to slaking our thirst. If when we came close to it we found something even better than water to drink, we might not have found what we were expecting to find, but we certainly would not complain. If we were to find a fountain of wine instead, in the sense of the wine of life, the blissful essential nectar of Enlightenment (*amṛta*), we would be so delighted with what we had found that we would forget the very idea of the water we once imagined it to be. Having given up our belief in the water, we do not think of what we have found as 'non-water'.

It is a little like the view that people might take of monks or hermits or anyone who adopts some kind of 'restricted' lifestyle – even temporarily as on retreat. People look at you and ask, 'What have you got? You have no career, no money, no TV, no decent clothes, no meat, no alcohol. Where's the fun in that?' There is no ready answer to this. Of course, monks usually seem happy enough, and people who go on retreat often say they have benefited hugely from the experience, but it is difficult to explain quite why or how that is the case in terms that people who have not experienced the situation for themselves will understand.

Chapter Six

Truths and illusions

Looking for the plantain's core

Just as there is nothing when
A banana tree with all its parts
Is torn apart, it is the same when a person
Is divided into the [six] constituents.

Therefore the Conquerors said,
'All phenomena are selfless.'
Since this is so, you must accept
All six constituents as selfless.

Thus neither self nor non-self
Are understood as real,
Therefore the Great Subduer rejected
The views of self and non-self.[62]

The banana tree is a well-known Buddhist simile. The plantain or banana tree does not have a solid core, being made up of layers like an onion, so that if you try to get at the essence of the banana tree by stripping off its successive layers, eventually you come to nothing at all. Likewise, when you practise the reflection on the six elements, stripping away earth, then water, fire, air, space, and finally consciousness, you end up with nothing.

It is the method of stripping away the various constituents that is the object of Nāgārjuna's attention here. It is essentially the Hīnayāna approach, and Nāgārjuna's criticism of it is that it does not take the process far enough. The truth of *anattā* (Pāli; Sanskrit *anātman*) is not just the absence of self in the obvious sense; it is the absence of self in anything whatsoever. The way we reify things, craving and resenting what we take to be permanent entities that can be grasped or pushed away, is a direct reflection of our belief in the fixed self. Therefore to regard the self as illusory, and the six constituents as real, is a pointless exercise.

> We must rely on relative truth for the purposes of clear thinking, to understand at least where absolute truth is not to be found.

Even the view of non-self is wrong inasmuch as it is a view, and therefore something to which the self becomes attached. There is no point in congratulating yourself on dispatching self-view when the view of non-self has become simply a more subtle self-view. The only way we can see through the self is to be, to some extent at least, free from attachment and hatred at the most subtle level. In order to understand any Buddhist doctrine properly we have to identify it as relative truth, and not take it as absolute truth. We have to rely on relative truth for the purpose of clear thinking, and in order at least to understand where absolute truth is not to be found; but this relative truth includes the understanding that ultimate truth can be neither thought about nor spoken about.

The limits of the world

> *Sights, sounds and so forth were said by the Subduer*
> *Neither to be true nor false;*
> *If from one position its opposite arises,*
> *Both in fact do not exist.*

Thus ultimately this world
Is beyond truth and falsehood,
Therefore he does not assert
That it really is or is not.

[Knowing that] these in all ways do not exist,
How could the All-Knower say
They have limits or no limits,
Or have both or neither?[63]

Those things which can be smelled, tasted, touched and thought, i.e. the objects of the senses, are said by the Buddha to be neither absolutely real nor absolutely unreal, and Nāgārjuna goes on to offer a logical explanation for this. His argument is that to exist absolutely means to exist independently, which is impossible

There is no question of space, of the universe, being finite or infinite, if we accept that space is an aspect of consciousness itself.

for anything that arises in dependence upon causes and conditions. If the existence of something necessarily involves the existence of its opposite, then that thing cannot be said to be absolutely real. Any conditioned thing comes into being in dependence upon that which it is not, upon its own non-existence. There is no life without death, no being without non-being, no light without darkness, no truth without falsehood, no craving without hatred, no absolute without the relative. And of course vice versa: if things are not absolutely real, they are not absolutely unreal either. Like a mirage, the world is there in a sense. Just as the mirage is there as an object of the sense of sight, so the world is experienced as being there; but it is not experienced as a really existing object.

Nāgārjuna goes on to refer to what are usually termed the fourteen 'inexpressibles'. These comprise four basic questions upon which the Buddha would not speak, which become fourteen on the basis of the formulaic ways in which they may

be addressed. Two of them are to do with our relationship
with the body. Thus the life principle (*jīva*) cannot be said
to be identical with the physical body (*rūpa*), nor entirely
separate from it. Four more questions deal with what happens
to a Buddha after his death or *parinirvāṇa*: it cannot be said
that he exists, or that he does not exist, or that he is both
existent and non-existent, or that he is neither existent nor
non-existent. All these four possibilities are inexpressible.
The other eight 'inexpressibles' concern whether or not the
universe is eternal, and whether or not it is infinite. 'Space'
cannot be said to be finite or limited in extent, nor can it be
said to be unlimited or infinite, nor both, nor neither. The
same goes for the question of whether or not the universe
is eternal.[64]

Of the fourteen questions, twelve illustrate the traditional
four alternative positions that can logically be taken with regard
to the metaphysical status of things. Thus, if it cannot be said
that the world has a limit, we must go on to propose that it
has no limit; and if neither of these positions can be upheld,
then we must posit that it is both limited and unlimited; and
if this position is also rejected, then we are left with the only
possibility open to us, that it is neither limited nor unlimited;
but this too is not the case.

The reality of conditioned existence, being dependent on
causes and conditions, cannot be said to be finite or infinite,
because if it has an existence that is only relative, like that of
a mirage, the question of its real existence doesn't arise. The
question of duration cannot apply to something that does not
have any substantial existence of its own in the first place. The
same may be said of the nature of space. It is generally held by
idealist philosophers that space is not a thing in the sense of
an empty box in which things are deposited. Space is a mode
of our perception. It is not so much part of what we see as
part of our perceptual apparatus, as is time. If we accept that
space is an aspect of consciousness itself, there is no question
of space, of the universe, being either finite or infinite.

From the Buddhist point of view, therefore, to try to ascertain whether the world is finite or infinite is quite mistaken; there is no question of its being either. One might say that while for certain practical purposes it is useful to assume that the universe is finite, for other practical purposes it is useful to assume that it is infinite. Scientists, for example, treat the universe as a discrete entity with boundaries of some kind, even though they may not be able to describe those boundaries in terms that can be understood except perhaps in terms of mathematics. On the other hand, philosophically speaking, however far the mind reaches out into the universe there must be further to go. But this is not to say that the universe as such is either finite or infinite, or indeed both, or even neither, because like any other conditioned thing it is not a self-existent reality.

The illusory elephant

'Innumerable Buddhas have come, will come and are
Here at present; there are tens of millions of sentient
Beings, but the Buddhas will abide
In the past, the present and the future;

The extinguishing of the world in the three
Times does not cause it to increase,
Then why was the All-Knower silent
About the limits of the world?'

That which is secret for a common
Being is the profound doctrine,
The illusory nature of the world,
The ambrosia of the Buddha's teaching.

Just as the production and the disintegration
Of an illusory elephant are seen,
But the production and disintegration
Do not really exist,

So the production and disintegration
Of the illusory world are seen,
But the production and disintegration
Ultimately do not exist.

Just as an illusory elephant,
But a bewildering of consciousness
Comes not from anywhere,
Goes not, nor really stays,

So this world of illusion,
A bewildering of consciousness,
Comes not from anywhere,
Goes not, nor really stays.

Thus it has a nature beyond time;
Other than as a convention
What world is there in fact
Which would be 'is' or 'is not'?

This is why the Buddha
At all times kept silent
About the fourfold format: with or
Without a limit, both or neither.[65]

Why did the Buddha stay silent on the subject of the end of the world?

The illusory elephant appears again and again in Buddhist philosophical literature. Just like the mirage, the elephant is not really there, it having been conjured up by a magician. But if the magician destroys the illusion he has produced, no elephant has been killed. The elephant did not exist in the first place, and it is impossible for anything that does not exist to be destroyed.

This, essentially, is Nāgārjuna's answer to an objection raised by certain philosophers of his time. The objection is based on the premise that there are no new sentient beings coming into existence, and that since innumerable Buddhas are dedicated to effecting their liberation from the world, which will decrease their numbers, eventually all beings must attain liberation. Now inasmuch as the conditioned world is the creation of conditioned consciousness, the world itself must eventually have an end: the world is made up of beings, thus no more beings, no more world. So why did the Buddha stay silent on the subject of the end of the world? There is a similar, more modern concern for anyone who contemplates the Buddhist doctrine of rebirth. In view of the population explosion in recent times, where do all the extra 'souls' come from? Do they come from another world, another planet, or another realm of being altogether?

According to Nāgārjuna, the world cannot really come to an end. Like the illusory elephant, since it never really came into existence, it cannot really go out of existence either. Having no real existence, it cannot be said to be either finite or infinite. In reality the world does not come from anywhere, does not go anywhere, and does not even stay. When we say that the world neither exists nor does not exist, we are thinking of its existence in space. But the reality of the world is beyond space. Similarly, the true nature of the world is also beyond time. It neither comes into existence nor passes out of existence. To say, 'the world exists,' or 'the world does not exist,' or 'the world will have an end,' is to speak in conventional terms. Such terms enable us to communicate with one another, but the concepts employed are not to be taken as having ultimate validity. For this reason the Buddha kept silent about the limits of the world. The nature of the world is beyond categorization. In the face of the intractable nature of objective truth with respect to such issues, silence is the appropriate attitude.

The Body of the Dharma

When the body, which is unclean,
Coarse, an object of the senses,
Does not stay in the mind [as unclean],
Although it is all the time in view,

Then how could this doctrine
Which is most subtle, profound,
Baseless and not manifest,
Appear with ease to the mind?

Realizing that this doctrine is too
Profound and hard to understand,
The Buddha, the Subduer,
Turned away from teaching it.

This doctrine wrongly understood
Ruins the unwise, because
They sink into the filth
Of nihilistic views.

Further, the stupid who fancy
Themselves wise, having a nature
Ruined by rejecting [emptiness] fall headfirst
To a fearful hell from their wrong understanding.

Just as one comes to ruin
Through wrong eating and obtains
Long life, freedom from disease,
Strength and pleasure through right eating,

So one comes to ruin
Through wrong understanding
But gains bliss and complete enlightenment
Through right understanding.[66]

We do not even see the true nature of our own physical body, with which we are in contact every moment of every day, so how can we be expected to see the true nature of the world, subtle and profound as this is? Elsewhere in the *Ratnamālā*, Nāgārjuna gives the traditional skilful means of viewing the body as impure or unlovely (*aśubha*). Suffice to say in this context that our inability to perceive the impurity of the body is cited here to illustrate the low level of awareness of the ordinary mind. It is as if to say that wisdom begins at home, where we live day by day, in the body.

Teachings like this run completely against the grain of our whole way of thinking and, more importantly, our whole way of being.

Given the enormous gulf in understanding between the ordinary everyday consciousness and the Enlightened consciousness, it is understandable that after his attainment of Enlightenment the Buddha was at first reluctant to teach the Dharma. So far as he was concerned in his newly Enlightened state, the truth of the nature of reality was incommunicable to ordinary people, deeply entrenched as they were in worldly ways.

He was not thinking of matters of morality and discipline, or even of meditation, hard though these things were for people to master. It was the truth of conditionality that the Buddha felt would be too great a challenge for ordinary people. Teachings like this run completely against the grain of our whole way of thinking and, more importantly, our whole way of being. Thus it was only at the prompting of the great deva Brahmā Sahampati, who reminded him that there were yet some beings 'with but a little dust in their eyes', that the Buddha changed his mind. What he did not change, however, was his belief that his teaching was supremely difficult to master.[67]

Having thoroughly exposed the general unreadiness of the ordinary mind for transcendental wisdom, Nāgārjuna warns of two dangerous extremes into which the unwise and unwary are liable to fall when they attempt to grasp the teaching. When you think you have understood it you are liable either to reject it, or else to accept it as a nihilistic teaching. To fall into either of these extremes is disastrous. Nāgārjuna elsewhere famously remarks that if you misunderstand the Śūnyavāda, the teaching of emptiness, you are like someone who is poisoned by the only medicine that can cure them of their sickness.[68] He takes a similar line here, as he returns to a consideration of the body, comparing the process of taking in food with that of taking in the teaching. It is significant that we naturally speak of 'digesting' information in the sense of absorbing it, making it ours, making it part of us. The information or teaching has to descend from the head into the heart and stomach, even into our limbs, into the way we move and act. And, in the case of both food and teachings, what we take in may nourish us, but it may poison us too.

This is perhaps surprising. We tend to think of the truth as purely objective and invariably beneficial. The important thing, we imagine, is to 'get our heads around it', as the saying is. But Nāgārjuna draws attention here to the fact that the truth needs the right 'vessel' before it can operate as Dharma. It is possible to take in the teaching in a way that causes delusion and suffering. An obvious example of misunderstanding the doctrine is literal-mindedness with respect to teachings like the Tathāgatagarbha, the 'womb of Enlightenment' doctrine. This teaching, which reminds us that Buddhahood is our true nature here and now, can be misunderstood as suggesting that we are already Enlightened and that to make any effort to attain Enlightenment is therefore deluded.

Sometimes we gobble down too much, or treat ourselves to teachings that are a little too rich for us. Sometimes we are simply not ready for theoretical teachings that require some preparatory understanding and practice. Another way to get indigestion is to take in different kinds of teaching which, though they may be nourishing when taken separately, are mutually incompatible. Different presentations of the doctrine, Zen and Shin for example, may be ultimately tending in the same direction, towards liberation, but they may take very different routes. Zen relies on 'self-power' (*jiriki*), whereas the devotional approach of Shin is a matter of dependence on 'other-power' (*tariki*), in which one surrenders any attempt to attain Enlightenment by one's own efforts and relies entirely on the compassion of Amitābha. The two paths have a common goal, and both involve complete commitment, but they will not work together.

Clarity

Therefore having forsaken all nihilistic
Views and rejections concerning emptiness,
Strive your best to understand correctly
For the sake of achieving all your aims.

If this doctrine is not truly understood,
The conception of an 'I' prevails,
Hence come virtuous and non-virtuous actions
Which give rise to good and bad rebirths.[69]

Nāgārjuna's final instruction in his account of the doctrines of definite goodness, before he returns to the subject of high status, is that we should try to understand the doctrines correctly. It might seem odd that this needed saying at all, let alone that it should form his final message to the king on the subject. But it serves to remind us that in our approach to the teaching many of us have a deep resistance to clarity. How far do we really want to expose ourselves to the clear light of the Dharma? Some people imagine that if they mean well, and have a vague idea of the teachings, that will be enough. They seem to imagine that it is somehow not in keeping with the spirit of the Dharma to be clear and precise in one's thinking, and that the rational mind should be left well out of it. Nāgārjuna is quite clear,

How far do we really want to expose ourselves to the clear light of the Dharma?

however, that if we do not understand the teaching correctly, we are not going to see through the conception of an 'I', of the self as a mere idea, to the true reality of things. If *śūnyatā* is not properly and clearly understood, the result is an ego-based life, whatever else we may do in the way of spiritual practice.

On the other hand, let us not take the word 'doctrine' too literally. It does not refer simply to conceptual formulations of the teaching as objects of intellectual understanding. To understand the doctrine means not just knowing the ideas but realizing the nature of voidness as an experience, a way of living. How much if anything you need to know about Buddhism to be a Buddhist and to realize something at least of the goal of Buddhism is an interesting question. It depends upon what one means by Buddhism, of course. Buddhism is whatever frees us from the grip of the ego, and you would be unlikely to get very far without the encouragement of others who have had at least some personal experience of the egoless state themselves. This means being involved in a tradition in which this teaching and this experience is familiar and accepted. But you do not need to know very much yourself, certainly not all the niceties of Madhyamaka philosophy.

Chapter Seven

An adventure
with no end in sight

Pleasure and pain

Although a Universal Monarch rules
Over the four continents, his pleasures
Are regarded as only two,
The physical and the mental.

Physical feelings of pleasure
Are only a lessening of pain.
Mental pleasures are made by thought,
Created only by the intellect.

All the wealth of worldly pleasures
Are but a lessening of suffering,
Or are only [creations of] thought,
Thus they are in fact not real.

One by one there is enjoyment of
Continents, countries, towns and homes,
Conveyances, seats, clothing, beds, food,
Drink, elephants, horses and women.

When the mind has any [one of these
As its object] there is said to be
Pleasure, but if no attention is paid to the others,
The others are not then, in fact, real [causes of pleasure].

When [all] five senses, eye and so forth,
[Simultaneously] apprehend their objects,
A thought [of pleasure] does not refer [to all of them],
Therefore at that time they do not all give pleasure.

Whenever any of the [five] objects is known
[As pleasurable] by one of the [five] senses,
Then the remaining [objects] are not so known
Since they are not real [causes of pleasure].[70]

Some religious texts talk about the need to give up worldly pleasure or happiness, but I would personally like to see people giving up their attachment to worldly misery.

By 'mental pleasures' Nāgārjuna means ambitions, plans, dreams, whether sleeping or waking, and entertainment (in our case, perhaps reading, listening to the radio, watching television, gambling and so on). They are ways in which we distract ourselves from the tedium of ordinary life. Advertisements, for example, are often designed to create mental pleasure. I was surprised once – though perhaps I should not have been – to discover that advertisements for summer holidays start appearing early in January. In the midst of winter one is tempted by thoughts of golden sands and palm trees, and this kind of happy anticipation helps to keep one going through the winter months. Such pleasure is not purely mental because it is largely an anticipation of physical pleasure. Even in the most refined of mental pleasures, like meditation or art, the pleasure is felt in the body. In the higher stages of meditation sense consciousness is inhibited, so that you may not hear or feel anything. But the sense of floating that this withdrawal from the senses seems to induce in the mind suggests that the connection between mind and body remains. Likewise, it is virtually impossible to enjoy physical pleasure that is unaccompanied by mental activity. Sexual pleasure is often bound up with mental projections, and being massaged may be valued for its effect on the mind as much as on the body. Perhaps the nearest one could get to a pure physical pleasure would be to drink, on a very hot day, a cup of very cold water.

However, in this section Nāgārjuna is concerned to show that pleasure and pain are less real than we assume. Firstly, universal monarchs for all their power have no greater capacity for pleasure than anyone else. They have just physical pleasure and mental pleasure. They have the same six senses as anyone else. However exquisite the pleasures you can enjoy, the organism can take only so much before it is surfeited.

The king has enormous choice, he has anything and everything at his disposal; but this wealth does not multiply his pleasure. Perhaps there are three or four thousand women in his harem; but he can enjoy only one of them at a time. The same goes for everything else he possesses. Just because he owns a thousand horses, it doesn't mean to say he *enjoys* a thousand horses. He can ride only one at a time. He may have a hundred shirts, but he can wear no more shirts than a man who owns just one. He might enjoy the thought that he possesses all those things, and that each day he wakes up with a different woman and puts on a new shirt. No doubt a man with one shirt would be very pleased to have another one. But the pleasure would not last. He would soon feel the same as he did before. A third shirt would give him nothing like the same pleasure. The more we acquire, the less enjoyment our 'pleasures' bring. In fact, they may bring worries. If you are wearing your only shirt, you know where it is – on your back. But if you have a hundred shirts, they need a lot of looking after; and one can imagine the difficulties of having a multitude of women all competing with one another for your favour. So the idea that multiplying our possessions multiplies our enjoyment is an illusion. It is understandable that we are fooled by it, but if we are mindful, and examine our experience closely, we should be able to see through the illusion.

The same principle applies to the five senses. When you enjoy something, you will rarely be experiencing the pleasure through more than one sense organ. You may try, but one sense will tend to predominate. Indeed, in a mix of pleasures, the different pleasures can distract from each other. Nāgārjuna's point is that when you are awake all five senses are functioning, but only one sense at a time experiences pleasure. The experience of the others is at best neutral, or even disagreeable. Two senses experiencing pleasure at the same time is probably the best we can hope for. The nineteenth-century cleric and wit Sydney Smith famously imagined heaven as being like eating pate de foie gras to the sound of trumpets, and perhaps he knew from experience that these particular pleasures complemented one another. However, in general, you cannot really concentrate on one pleasure without the other being a distraction. Your enjoyment of a beautiful piece of music, for instance, may be spoiled by a sudden bad smell or a draught.

A late nineteenth-century French novel, *Against Nature*, (*À Rebours*, by J.K. Huysmans), explores this theme. Its hero, Des Esseintes, isolates himself in his castle from the pleasures and pains of the world outside, and tries to make sure that everything within the castle is perfectly adapted to his enjoyment. Everything is uniquely beautiful; everything has just the right smell and the right taste and makes the right sound. He rids himself of anything that is not perfectly agreeable to him. Of course, all he is doing is increasing his sensitivity, thus making himself more susceptible to pain. In the end his scheme of pleasure breaks down, and he cannot enjoy anything.

Sometimes we have an experience of intense pleasure, but the intensity is necessarily fleeting. We get used to the pleasure, for the senses are quite quickly jaded. There were ancient kings who did their best to make the most of the immense variety of pleasures available to them, and who virtually destroyed themselves in the process. They couldn't sustain it. In such circumstances the whole psycho-physical organism starts resisting. It seems to have been a source of human frustration in all ages, even to the present day, that we can only enjoy one thing at a time, and that we cannot even enjoy that one thing for very long. Yet few of us are prepared to accept the evidence for this fact.

One is quickly surfeited, even by the most refined aesthetic pleasure. For instance, if you go to a large art gallery, you may very much enjoy the first room, and perhaps the second, but after that, even though the paintings are extremely beautiful, and though you may have come a long way to see them, you cannot take in any more. You just want to go and have a cup of coffee. It can be quite a disappointment, like realizing at a feast that you have no room for the delicious dessert.

Culture-guzzling package holidays represent our unwillingness to acknowledge this reality. People say, 'I saw this famous old church. Now was it in Paris or was it Berlin? I guess it might have been Amsterdam.' For them, everything beautiful merges into one vaguely stimulating but rather exhausting experience. They can remember occasional details, but not necessarily what it was or where it was, or even why they saw it. All they really know is that it cost them a lot of money. This is why they take so many photographs. They hope to have the leisure when they get home to take in the sights that they didn't have time to look at when they were actually there.

There is a certain self-delusion that lurks in our consumption of pleasure. How often, for example, is one really carried away by a piece of music or a painting or poem? I suspect that such pleasures are more elusive than most of us care to admit. We have to be in a certain mood. Having had an intense aesthetic experience once, we expose ourselves again and again to the kind of work that produced it originally, and declare how much we like it. But more often than not, we are just not in the mood to appreciate it fully. It is clear that some people have a greater capacity for enjoying the arts than others, but even in their case the enjoyment is limited. Should you read poetry all day, even, you might get perhaps no more than two or three moments of aesthetic exhilaration from it.

Even meditation, while it can be genuinely and deeply pleasurable, does not guarantee pleasure every time you practise it. You may be feeling a strong – even a blissful – positive emotion, but you may also be aware that your knee is hurting or your back is aching. You may also experience an unaccountable urge to get up and end the meditation, as though a gravitational pull was exerting itself. What does this say about our relationship with pleasure? How comfortable are we with it? Most people rarely experience true ecstasy. To be able to feel intense pleasure and joy, you have to have a certain amount of energy bubbling up within you. It is not going to come from the pleasurable objects themselves. At our best, most of us feel moderately content most of the day with, if we are lucky, a few gentle highlights when we feel quite good – but our experience of pleasure usually doesn't go much beyond this. A retreat with others is usually our best chance of achieving a markedly higher level of happiness than we can manage in ordinary life, and this seems to be mainly a matter of collective energies bubbling over. It is always good to see such high spirits on a retreat, even if the mood is not exactly one of spiritual exaltation. Such ordinary, innocent happiness is rare enough.

Some people, of course, carefully cultivate their itches for the sake of the satisfaction they get from scratching them. This is called being devoted to a life of pleasure.

Some religious texts talk about the need to give up worldly pleasure or happiness, but I would personally like to see people giving up their attachment to worldly misery. I would like to see them enjoying more of the simple pleasures of life. Many of those who are supposed to be wallowing in worldly pleasure, and who have everything at their command, tend to look miserable, gaunt, and even irritable.

So far, so uncontroversial. But can it be true that all bodily pleasures are no more than a lessening of pain? Is there no possibility of pure, unadulterated pleasure? It may seem unlikely, but this is the case. What we take for pleasure is only a slight amelioration of pain. Underlying any pleasure is a substratum of *dukkha*, the basic unsatisfactoriness of conditioned existence. Whether or not we acknowledge it, we have an uninterrupted baseline of negative feeling that never altogether goes away. A weekend break might seem like an opportunity to forget your troubles, but at the back of your mind will be some unresolved crisis at the office, or some problem with the neighbours at home, and the thought of that may never really leave you all through the weekend.

Even without any obvious cause for concern to keep us from being absorbed in a pleasurable situation, our pleasure is necessarily limited. Unless you are mindful of the fact that it is impermanent, your pleasure will entail a painful limitation of your being anyway, inasmuch as you are unconsciously holding that awareness of impermanence at bay all the time. You can enjoy that object fully only by limiting your mindfulness. This is difficult for us to appreciate; we cannot be aware of that limitation if we have never experienced what it is to be without it. Nevertheless, it produces a quietly uncomfortable or uneasy feeling at the back of the mind that cannot be banished.

We might conclude that there can be no completely unalloyed physical pleasure because all pleasure is a distraction from the basic unsatisfactoriness or inadequacy of conditioned existence. You obtain something that you have looked forward to for a long time, and even while you are enjoying it, there is deep in your consciousness the feeling that after all it is not as enjoyable as you had thought it would be. You eat, for example, to alleviate the pain of hunger, and much of the pleasure involved is in achieving this end. Any particularly strong desire can be quite painful, because insofar as you are not getting what you want there is an element of frustration in it. You acquire the desired object not because you really want it but rather to assuage the desire for it. This is not really true enjoyment.

Goethe's *Faust* provides a dramatic illustration of what Nāgārjuna is saying. Mephistopheles strikes a bargain with Faust by which he promises to give Faust any object of enjoyment, any power or pleasure he wants. He is able, for example, to give him Helen of Troy, the most beautiful woman who ever lived. The bargain is that if Faust ever said, 'Stop, this is a totally satisfying experience!' his soul would then go to Mephistopheles. But of course Faust is never able to say that. He never does find anything so completely satisfying or enjoyable that he wants it to last forever; so Mephistopheles fails to win his wager and consequently loses Faust's soul. This is a parable of human desire, showing that it cannot be satisfied by anything mundane. There is always some fly in the ointment, some imperfection, to any experience. Feelings of pleasure do exist, but they are only the scratching of an itch: it may be pleasant to scratch the itch but it is better not to have the itch at all.

In general, the more creative you are the more easily bored you get and the less easily distracted you are.

We have all experienced this frustration in one connection or another. The trick is to notice what the experience of pleasure really consists in, moment by moment. As you are planning some kind of pleasure for yourself, as well as when you are actually experiencing the pleasure, notice the pleasant feeling when it arises together with any accompanying unpleasant feeling. Notice even the resistance to examining your experience so closely, and any resistance to the idea of losing the craving for pleasure.

All this is not to say that we should stop craving pleasure. According to Buddhism, we just have to wake up to the fact that our craving for pleasure is in vain, because we don't enjoy our pleasures as truly and fully as we imagine we do. We scratch the old itch a bit, that's all. Some people, of course, carefully cultivate their itches for the sake of the satisfaction they get from scratching them. This is called being devoted to a life of pleasure.

How unsatisfactory desire can feel can be gauged by considering our more obviously neurotic cravings, those emerging out of a dull feeling of frustration, boredom, and emptiness. We look for something pleasurable in order to fill that void and relieve the boredom, at least partially and temporarily. You eat a chocolate or drink a cup of tea or put on a piece of music not so much for the positive enjoyment of such things but more because you don't know what else to do. It is these kinds of craving that should concern us most, more than those that arise out of a strong, healthy appetite. And the way to deal with them is to regard the boredom itself as a positive opportunity. It is like having to deal with fear, anger, or indeed craving, or any other negative mental state. It is an opportunity to experience the energy that is usually drained away by distractions. When you are really bored, the best thing you can do is sit down and let yourself experience the boredom more fully. It may not be a deep or satisfying state, but at least you are not indulging in the things with which you usually cover up this kind of experience. Your real state of mind is more nakedly exposed, because for the time being there are no distractions. If you can stay with the experience of boredom, you can try to feel your way through into something deeper, truer and more spontaneous within yourself.

This is likely to be more helpful than trying to force a more positive state into being or rushing to alleviate the boredom with a distraction. After a while you should find that the boredom passes. You will start to feel more positive simply by virtue of experiencing yourself more truly. And feeling more positive, you will probably want to get on with actually doing something positive. But if the minute you start feeling bored you turn on the radio or pick up the newspaper or ring somebody up, then you've lost the opportunity with which the boredom has presented you.

Boredom is an intermediate state between being in touch with deeper and truer levels within oneself and just being distracted. For the time being you're neither the one nor the other – hence the feeling of emptiness. You are neither really in touch with yourself nor being distracted from the fact that you are not really in touch with yourself. You have neither a truer, deeper enjoyment, nor a superficial enjoyment. At such a time, you can either rush into a superficial, transitory enjoyment, or else you can wait for true enjoyment to arise from within. Usually the state of boredom will not last more than a few hours.

There are, though, two different kinds of situation in which boredom arises. First, there is the boredom of not having anything to do, in which case you may end up asleep. It can take a lot of energy to hold yourself back from going in search of distractions, but just by falling asleep you will be refreshing yourself from deeper resources within you. Second, there is the boredom of doing something you find uninteresting. You may be working hard, but there are significant strata of your mind that are not engaged in what you are doing. The work itself is not a distraction and at the same time it prevents you from distracting yourself with something else. Whether in such a case you should carry on working or stop in order to gather together some more positive energies depends on circumstances, on how objectively important the work is.

Nothing is intrinsically boring. Anything can be boring if you have to do it all the time, but the same thing can be interesting when done occasionally, and quite restful when done more regularly. When you are not actively stimulated by what you are doing, you can occupy yourself with your own thoughts or just experience your own general positivity. But not for eight hours a day. Everyone needs a balance of relatively undemanding activity and more challenging, interesting work. When the balance is wrong, stress or boredom is the result. Where this balance lies depends on the individual. In general, the more creative you are, the more easily bored you get and the less easily distracted you are from that boredom. A dull, unimaginative person is less easily bored and by the same token more tolerant of distraction. Give some people piped music, cups of tea, and a bit of a chat at intervals, and they can do repetitive work year after year.

Boredom is connected with not being able to express your energies. When someone starts talking to you, for example, you might be quite interested in what they are saying, but if they ramble on and on, and give you no opportunity to respond, you will probably start to feel bored. Your energy is being frustrated. Boredom is also connected with not being able to be yourself. You start feeling bored when too little of yourself is involved in what you are doing. When work is too repetitive to stimulate your energies, you are being prevented, effectively, from being fully involved. You are drying up inside; there is an empty space where there should have been an active, spontaneous individual. If you were a young civil servant and you got an important and complicated directive from higher up, you might have a lot of fun working out how to implement it. But if after a few years the inventive, creative part of yourself stopped being involved, you might well start to find the work boring.

Once you start analyzing things in this way, you may begin wondering whether you have ever experienced real pleasure. If you arrive home from a day's outing and someone asks, 'Did you have a good time?', unless the day was a disaster you will probably reply, 'Yes, I really enjoyed it.' But did you? No doubt doing something different is refreshing, but when you think about the day in detail, you will probably find it to have been, like most things, a mixed experience. We give the label 'pleasure' to certain experiences perhaps because they involve giving way to certain appetites, or even merely spending money, and we don't like to question the label because then we would have to change our ideas about life.

The bias of memory

When the mind apprehends a past object
Which has been picked up by the senses,
It imagines and fancies
It to be pleasurable.[71]

Because we want to experience pleasure rather than pain, we naturally and automatically edit the past when we think about it.

As adults, most of us look back to our childhood as a time of innocent happiness. Children are told that schooldays are the happiest time of their lives. Children themselves, of course, may take a different view. They think, reasonably enough, that they will be happy when they are grown up and able to do what they want to do, when they can eat all the chocolate they like and play all day and never be told to go to bed and not have to wash their necks.

Nostalgia, or a sentimental dwelling on the past, is the way we create pleasure out of past unhappiness. The past is all the more pleasurable, the further we are away from it. We settle down in the past, consolidating our identity more and more round it as we feed our attachment to what we are remembering. We choose the past over the present or the future, trying to console or compensate ourselves for the present by turning over in our mind the supposed joys of the past.

Different people have different attachments. Some people are nostalgic, some people live for the present in a very narrow, mindless way, while others live for the pleasures of the future. One of the benefits of going on spiritual retreat is that the past and future both fade into the background. What you have been worrying about seems much less important; what you are going back to and what you will be doing there seem like another world. You are in the present not in the sense of being lost in the concerns of the present, but in the sense of being simply aware.

Our natural tendency is to soften or even forget the harsher features of the past. If we took a more clear-eyed view of it, though, we would have to contemplate a less rosy, more painful reality. As this would become our present experience for as long as we continued to think of the past, it would make our present experience itself more painful. Because we want to experience pleasure rather than pain, we naturally and automatically edit the past when we think about it. Not all our painful experiences can be edited out so easily, but this editing process works on many of the disagreeable details of our lives.

You may even come to see a painful situation in the past as so positively pleasurable that you start thinking of revisiting it. Forgetting the lesson that this situation has taught you, you turn the pain into a sort of wistful melancholy. A certain fascination about that difficult situation lures you back into it and you can end up going through much the same thing all over again, if under slightly different circumstances.

In this connection it could be helpful to keep a diary, which would give you a counterweight of evidence against the sweetening bias of memory. The positive and pleasant experiences would take their natural place amongst the more difficult ones, and in this context pleasant memories could achieve a more truly Proustian poignancy and intensity. In his great novel *In Search of Lost Time* Proust's narrator recounts various intensely joyful moments in his childhood, which he re-experiences through little events or accidents in his mature life. But he doesn't bathe these memories in a warm glow. There are equally intense painful experiences, from which an adult is no less excluded than he is from the pleasures of childhood. Proust writes, 'The true paradises are the paradises that one has lost.' And he says of the life of the Duchess of Guermantes, that it 'appeared to me to be a paradise I would never enter'.

However, the re-experiencing of a moment in childhood (rather than merely remembering it) produces a sort of transcendence of time and space in one's mind. It is that transcendence that is the real joy, not the rosy misapprehension of a particular time in one's life. It is worth considering that this transcendence of time and space does in fact take us closer to how things really are. For example, from reading the *Udāna* or some of the other books of the Pāli canon one can get a vivid sense of the Buddha as he may actually have appeared to people, and of what life in the early days of Buddhism may have been like. I have occasionally had an odd feeling of being in very much the same sort of situation as some of the early disciples of the Buddha. Once, when I was in New Zealand, I found myself wandering in a remote part of the country, in the company of a few friends, and talking with them about the Dharma as if it were something just revealed to mankind. I had a slightly uncanny but powerful sense of the millennia between me and those original followers of the Buddha just falling away. In such cases one can feel that one is not just imagining something taking place, but that one is actually present. You can be meditating, and it might as well be the fourth or fifth century BCE; and when you open your eyes there is a moment perhaps before your personal historical location swims back into perception.

If you do recapture some vivid experience from your earlier life, a question arises. Given that your experience repeats, at least momentarily, your experience then, where are you? Are you there or are you here? In that moment you cannot tell. You are both here *and* there. In that sense, or to that extent, you transcend time. When you experience what you experienced as a child, given that it is a child's experience, are you now a child or are you an adult? You are of course both, and neither. In a sense you have transcended time. Your experience momentarily bridges the past and the present, giving you a strange impression that time is illusory. It is as though your experience contains the past and the present.

Allowing our imagination to link us directly with past and even future ages can be a useful exercise, helping us to break out of the cocoon of the present, and out of our tendency to identify completely with our present situation. Wherever we may now find ourselves, we can reflect on what we would see and hear around us if we were to go back a hundred years, or a thousand years, or even ten million years. Where we are walking may even have once been under the sea. Reflections like this can take away the ground from under our feet and remind us that the world we see is not the fixed reality we take it for.

The permanent possibility of sensation

Also the one sense which here [in the world
Is said to] know one object,
Without an object is as unreal
As that object is without it.

Just as a child is said to be born
Dependent on a father and mother,
So a consciousness is said to arise
Dependent on a sense and on a form.[72]

It is a basic Buddhist tenet that, as the second of these two verses reminds us, consciousness is conditioned. It arises from the interaction of the senses with their respective objects, which themselves arise in dependence upon consciousness as well as on each other. From this the Abhidharma concludes that there is a consciousness for every sense organ. Thus 'eye consciousness' arises in dependence on the contact of the organ of sight with

Matter is not an entity that is there all the time, waiting to be perceived. It is the permanent possibility of that sort of experience occurring.

the visual object. The Abhidharma lists first the six senses (including the mind in the ordinary sense of the term), then the twelve *āyatanas* or 'bases', which are the six senses and their respective objects. Finally, it enumerates the eighteen *dhātus* or 'spheres', which comprise both senses and objects together with their corresponding consciousnesses.[73]

In the case of the visual sense, the eye perceives an object of a certain shape and colour. Without an object for it to perceive that sense organ ceases to be a sense organ. Conversely, there can be no object of perception without a perceiving sense organ. This is why John Stuart Mill defined matter as the permanent possibility of sensation.[74] Matter is not an entity that is there all the time, waiting to be perceived. It is the permanent possibility of that sort of experience occurring when a sense organ comes into contact with its appropriate object.

There is no object without a subject. There is no subject without an object. Neither exists independently. So if a thing cannot exist except in dependence on some other thing, can it be said truly to exist at all? If the object of sight can exist only in relation to the sense organ of sight, and vice versa, can either of them be said to be real? Here we come back to *śūnyatā* or emptiness: each is 'empty' of independent existence, and hence is only relatively real. And if the production of pleasure is dependent on these unreal sense organs and their unreal objects, how can the pleasure itself be real?

No time like the present

> *Past and future objects*
> *And the senses are unreal,*
> *So too are present [objects] since*
> *They are not distinct from these two.*[75]

Nāgārjuna goes on to undermine our belief in pleasure by questioning its temporal context. Past, present and future objects all depend upon one another, so that they are only relatively real. They are not real in themselves. The notion that things are in the past is dependent upon the notion that they were once in the present and before that they were in the future. The future, by virtue of its being the future, will become the past. Present objects are of the same conditioned nature as past and future objects, since the present moment can always be subdivided. The present is only a moving boundary or edge between the past and the future. It is where the two edges meet: it does not have an independent existence. The present is the term we apply to our experience of the future continually becoming past. To talk of being 'in the now' really means being out of time altogether. There is no 'now' where one can be. We say 'all the time' but that makes no sense either. One can accumulate as much of nothing as one likes; it will all add up to nothing.

> You cannot be anywhere other than here and now, but nor can you really even be here and now. There is no 'being' at any point in time at all.

If the present does not exist, the past does not exist either, because what is past is made up of what was once present. The same goes for the future, because the future is made up of what will be present. Every past was once a present; every future will be a present. Nāgārjuna is trying to bring us to an experience of time as unreal: he says that the present is unreal because, as he has already shown, past and future are unreal. One can also say that past and future are unreal because the present is unreal, since this amounts to the same thing.

How, asks Nāgārjuna, can a real pleasure arise from unreal senses and their unreal sense objects? Whether in the past, present or future, the pleasure cannot be grasped or secured in any way. There is nothing there. You cannot be anywhere other than here and now, but nor can you really even be here and now. There is no 'being' at any point in time at all. The now that is the only point at which you can be is outside time, and therefore outside any sense of a subject as opposed to an object. There is no 'you' there, and therefore no 'being'.

The thought that pleasure is unreal, though at the same time basically frustrating or painful, helps to free us from our attachment to it, and it is at this point that we realize that pain too is unreal. This is unlikely to happen the other way round. Trying to take pain as unreal while taking pleasure as real can only be a self-serving fantasy, as a result of which we dig ourselves deeper into self-delusion. If pleasure is grasped at as a self-existent reality, pain will feel if anything even more real.

Living in the present is good, but with the arising of insight one realizes that strictly speaking there is no present moment in which to live, and that one cannot live in time at all. And one can only live beyond time when one is not affected by either pleasure or pain. Without repressing your feelings, without being alienated, you learn to treat pleasure and pain as being the same, and therefore do not react to them.

Thus, being in the present is not a matter of grasping at the present. It is about not anticipating the future or hanging onto the past. Its concern is with how we see ourselves. If we say 'This is me, this is how I am, take me as I am,' we are limiting ourselves by identifying with what we are now. We are not prepared to respond *creatively* to the present.

Chasing moving shadows

Just as due to error the eye perceives
A [whirling] firebrand as a wheel,
So the senses apprehend
Present objects [as if real].

The senses and their objects are regarded
As being composed of the elements,
Since the individual elements
Are unreal, so too are those objects.

If each element is different,
It follows that there could be fire without fuel.
If mixed they would be characterless
And this is true of the other elements.

Because the elements are unreal in both
These ways so too is composition,
Because composition is unreal
So too in fact are forms.

Also because consciousness, feelings,
Discriminations and factors of composition each
Are not self-existent realities in any way,
[Pleasures] are not ultimately real.

Just as a lessening of pain
Is fancied to be real pleasure,
So a suppression of pleasure
Is also fancied to be pain.

Thus attachment to finding pleasure
And to separating from pain
Are to be abandoned because they do not inherently
Exist; thereby for those who see thus there is liberation.[76]

Illustrations like that of the whirling firebrand, which we
have already met in this text, do not prove anything; they just
make clearer something that is independently known. The
image itself is clear enough. One whirls a firebrand around
to give an impression of a wheel of fire. But is what one sees
really a wheel of fire? No, one has created an illusion of one.
The eye is deceived by the speed of the firebrand's circular
motion. The real issue, though, is what this image is meant
to illustrate. Except in the case of simple illusions like this
one, how else do we experience present objects in a way that
we know them not to be? After all, the image is striking because

it is taken as anomalous. How do we get from this particular anomaly to a general rule that 'the senses apprehend present objects as if real' when they are illusory?

We have to look into things a bit more deeply, see what is really going on, see through our assumptions. Is there anything that is not in the process of changing, decaying, from one moment to the next? As with the wheel of fire, we know intellectually what is happening, but because we do not actually perceive what is going on, we happily ignore what we know to be true. And when we finally have to face the truth, we become downcast. It is as if we went about with our eyes half closed, allowing ourselves to be mesmerized.

Real satisfaction is what we would call 'lasting satisfaction', which is impossible, because 'lasting' means continuing within time, and time involves change.

Still trying to convince the king of the unreality of his pleasures, Nāgārjuna then breaks the senses and their objects down into their constituent elements: earth, water, fire, air, space, and consciousness. Those pleasures cannot be any more real than the elements out of which they are composed. Nāgārjuna is saying that you cannot distinguish the elements from one another completely; the element fire cannot have an independent existence from the element earth. Fire needs the earth element (and the air element, for that matter) as its fuel. On the other hand, if they were mixed together they would lose their specific characteristics. Hence they are neither different from one another, nor the same. Our pleasures are made up of nothing beyond these elements, which disappear when they are looked at closely. Out of these unreal elements we make our unreal sense organs and sense objects. And these unreal sense organs and sense objects produce an unreal consciousness – and an unreal pleasure.

What do we mean when we say that one thing is composed out of other things? Here Nāgārjuna asserts that the idea of composition itself is untenable. Can we really say that the wheel of fire is 'composed' of a moving firebrand? No, because time is unreal, fire is unreal, and – as Nāgārjuna has proved elsewhere (at least to his own satisfaction) – movement is impossible as well. 'Composition' suggests a number of things put together to form a whole. But a lot of nothing still adds up to nothing. Yet we insist on reifying even the most obviously insubstantial aspects of our experience. Is ignorance or attachment something that we can get rid of, or something we just have to drop? Ignorance is simply a word. If there really was such a thing as ignorance it could not be removed. One can only get rid of ignorance because it is not there. One can drop one's attachment because one is not holding onto it. The same goes for pleasure (and pain).

For the experience of pleasure to be possible in any real sense, there must be a real framework within which that experience can take place. And Nāgārjuna has been concerned to show the unreality of the framework within which pleasure is considered to be experienced in order to cast doubt on the reality of that pleasure. Demolish the framework, and the pleasure also collapses. The spiritual life, by contrast, *is* a real framework. Or, to put it another way, one could say that real satisfaction is possible only outside time. Of course, such satisfaction is not what we imagine it to be. Real satisfaction is what we would call 'lasting satisfaction', which is impossible because 'lasting' means continuing within time, and time involves change. Lasting satisfaction is possible only outside time, where the question of its lasting does not arise.

Abstruse and over-ingenious as these arguments may seem, such mental gymnastics were highly appreciated in ancient India. It seems that the Buddha's down-to-earth, common-sense approach was superseded quite early on by such dialectics. I have certainly had the experience myself in India of having to field quite intellectual questions from orthodox Brahmins. No doubt Nāgārjuna grew up with this mind-set, as he was formerly an orthodox Brahmin himself. But generally speaking, unlike Nāgārjuna, the super-subtle Brahmin tends to remain a Brahmin, with all his prejudices intact.

Those of us who are fortunate enough to be more simple-minded still manage to offer considerable resistance to the reality that Nāgārjuna is uncovering here. Just as we take a temporary and partial relief from pain to be pleasure, we also take a surrender of pleasure to be pain. We imagine that giving up the imaginary pleasures with which we alleviate our fundamentally painful existence must itself be painful. In fact, though, our predominant feeling may well be one of relief, freedom, and release from the sense of being in thrall to our desires – certainly in the long run.

Nāgārjuna's argument is meant to be a challenge to the importance of the place that pleasure and pain hold in our ordinary lives. Most of the time, if not all the time, we are instinctively searching for what is pleasurable and trying to separate ourselves from what is painful. We are probably not aware of the extent to which we do this. But unconsciously, we build our lives around these two things, making all sorts of adjustments and arrangements, taking all sorts of steps and measures, to ensure that we continue to experience as much pleasure and contentment and as little suffering and difficulty as possible, almost regardless of other considerations.

Because pleasure and pain do not inherently exist Nāgārjuna is suggesting that a life that is oriented towards finding pleasure and avoiding pain is one that is not oriented towards reality; it is therefore an unreal life – the conditioned in pursuit of the conditioned. It is a chasing after moving shadows. Such a life, he says, should be abandoned. At least, we need to reduce the extent to which these two drives dominate our lives. Making the pursuit of pleasure and the avoidance of pain one's overriding priority means that one is considering pleasure and pain to be more real than they actually are. A life of this kind is therefore based on unreality.

No mind

What sees [reality]? Conventionally they say
It is the mind, for without mental factors
There can be no mind, and [a second mind],
Because unreal, cannot be simultaneous.

Knowing thus truly and correctly
That animate beings are unreal,
Not being subject [to rebirth] and without grasping, one
Passes [from suffering] like a fire without its cause.

Bodhisattvas also who have seen it thus,
Seek perfect enlightenment with certainty,
They maintain a continuity of existence
Until enlightenment only through their compassion.[77]

When we assume that it is the mind that cognizes the nature of reality, we are thinking of the mind defined as 'awareness of an object', not as defined in any other way. But how do you know that it is the mind that sees the object, let alone that it sees reality? What you need is a 'second mind' to see the first mind, and see that it does in fact see reality. However, this requires a third mind to see the second, and a fourth to see the third, and so on. The search for such certainty is a fruitless regression to infinity. Consequently, it is only in a manner of speaking that one says that the mind sees reality. Mind itself cannot be considered to be an existent entity: it is a complex of a number of mental factors. If the mind is unreal, there is no question of its perceiving an object, least of all of its perceiving reality, nor even of a second mind seeing it doing so. Conventionally we see and

By the light by which the mind perceives its object, you can see that the mind is perceiving its object. A second mind is surplus to requirements. Hence the mind is said to be 'self-luminous'.

speak dualistically, in terms of subject and object. It is the only way in which it is possible for us to speak. Reality, therefore, unless it is thought of as dualistic, cannot be described as a subject or, as here, as an object of perception.

A point that Nāgārjuna does not make is that you no more need a second mind in order to perceive the fact that the first mind perceives than you need a second light to show you that the light you have in the first place is giving light. It is by the light given by the original light that you see *that* it is giving light. By the light by which the mind perceives its object, you can see *that* the mind is perceiving its object. A second mind is surplus to requirements. Hence the mind is said to be 'self-luminous'.

One of the implications of the refutation of a self-existent mind is that the so-called living being (*jīva*) lacks a basis in reality. If you can absorb this truth without falling into nihilism – that is, without losing the thread of compassion that binds you to beings – you are a bodhisattva. It is not that you regard living beings as absolutely non-existent, but you regard yourself and others as having a relative and contingent existence. In other words, by its very nature any kind of existence, as we are able to understand it, is relative. When one sees things in this way one is free from grasping, and therefore no longer subject to rebirth. There is no one there to do the grasping.

What the Bodhisattvas are certain of is their goal. They are certain that there is such a thing as Enlightenment, because they have already had some preliminary glimpses of it in the form of some Insight into the truth of non-ego. They have seen that a higher Transcendental dimension is attainable. They then hold back from arriving at the goal out of compassion for other beings. This is the popularized if dualistic Mahāyāna view that the Bodhisattva, in Dr Matics' phrase, 'hovers between being and non-being'. That is, he or she holds back from becoming completely immersed in *nirvāṇa* without, of course, becoming completely immersed in *saṃsāra*. He or she keeps in contact with *nirvāṇa*, with the ultimate spiritual dimension, through wisdom, and keeps in contact with *saṃsāra*, continuing the series of births and rebirths, through compassion. In a deeper sense the Bodhisattva has passed beyond the duality between *saṃsāra* and *nirvāṇa*. There is no question of their deciding, through compassion, to continue existing. They see no difference between remaining in the *saṃsāra* and not remaining in it. For them, wisdom and compassion, *nirvāṇa* and *saṃsāra*, are one.

In Tibet many lamas were believed to be Bodhisattvas who remained in the world and did not enter into *nirvāṇa* so that they could help other living beings. It was also believed that they could be identified when young and brought back to their original monasteries. But one must distinguish here between two kinds of rebirth. According to orthodox Buddhist belief, everybody is reborn, including great lamas. In theory one could go out and identify any child as having been a specific person in his or her previous life. But only a few of these rebirths can be of Bodhisattvas. When you identify a child as having been an abbot who died a few years before, it does not follow that he is necessarily an 'incarnate bodhisattva'. If that abbot himself was a bodhisattva then yes, the little boy will be a bodhisattva, but if the abbot was not a bodhisattva, the little boy will not be one either.

I was talking once to Christmas Humphreys about these 'reincarnate' lamas or *tulkus* and something he said seemed to sum up the plain facts of the situation in many cases. He remarked, 'I don't know what all the fuss is about incarnate lamas. What are they, after all? They're just the Buddhist equivalent of the local vicar reborn.' In the West we are very impressed if someone is presented as being the thirteenth incarnation of such and such an abbot of such and such a monastery; and the fact that the line has been maintained over many centuries, the lama being rediscovered over and over again, is no doubt impressive. But it does not necessarily mean that he is an incarnate bodhisattva. Remembering details of a previous life is certainly no guarantee of spiritual attainment. Dhardo Rinpoche once told me that it was his personal opinion, and the belief of quite a number of other lamas, that in Tibet there were among the two thousand officially recognized *tulkus* no more than six or seven, or at the most eight, who really were incarnate bodhisattvas.

A bodhisattva is one in whom the *bodhicitta* has arisen. An incarnate bodhisattva would be someone who had reached the eighth *bhūmi*, where the renunciation of *nirvāṇa* for oneself becomes a real possibility, and that is a very advanced stage indeed. Nāgārjuna himself, according to one tradition, was a bodhisattva of the second *bhūmi*. So one sees how difficult it is to be an incarnate bodhisattva.

It is a question of how deep our understanding of the nature of reality goes, of how 'intuitive' it becomes. And the way to deepen our understanding is to remind ourselves constantly that any understanding we do have has its limitations. After all, once our understanding has matured a little, we look back on our former confidence and think, 'How could I ever have kidded myself that I understood *that*? I didn't understand it at all.' We need the imagination to be able to project that mature reflection into a possible future in which our present knowledge will appear just as jejune. The spiritual life is an adventure with no end in sight. When we say, 'Now, finally, I understand,' we are really only just beginning.

Chapter Eight

....

To end as we began

A Sevenfold Pūjā

Therefore in the presence of an image
Or reliquary or something else
Say these twenty stanzas
Three times every day.

Going for Refuge with all forms of respect
To the Buddhas, excellent doctrine,
Supreme Community and Bodhisattvas
I bow down to all that is worthy of honour.

From all sins I will turn away
And thoroughly maintain all virtues,
I will admire all the merits
Of all embodied beings.

With bowed head and clasped hands
I petition the perfect Buddhas
To turn the wheel of doctrine and remain
As long as beings transmigrate.

Through the merit of having done all this and through
The merit that I have done and that I will do
May all sentient beings aspire
To the highest enlightenment.

May all sentient beings have all the stainless
Powers, freedom from all conditions of non-leisure,
Freedom of action
And good livelihood.

May all embodied beings
Have jewels in their hands and may
All the limitless necessities of life remain
Unconsumed as long as there is cyclic existence.

May all beings always be
[Born] as superior humans,
May all embodied beings have
Wisdom and the support [of ethics].

May embodied beings have a good complexion,
Good physique, great beauty, a pleasant appearance,
Freedom from disease,
Power and long life.

May all be skilled in the means [to extinguish
Suffering], and have liberation from it,
Absorption in the Three Jewels,
And the great wealth of Buddha's doctrine.

May they be adorned with love, compassion, joy,
Even-mindedness [devoid of] the afflictions,
Giving, ethics, patience, effort,
Concentration and wisdom.

May they have the brilliant major and minor marks
[of a Buddha]
From having finally completed the two collections
[of merit and wisdom]
And may they cross without interruption
The ten inconceivable stages.

May I also be adorned completely
With those and all other good qualities,
Be freed from all defects and possess
Superior love for all sentient beings.

May I perfect all the virtues
For which all embodied beings hope
And may I always relieve
The sufferings of all sentient beings.

May those beings in all worlds
Who are distressed through fear
Become entirely fearless
Through merely hearing my name.

Through seeing or thinking of me
Or only hearing my name may beings attain great joy,
Naturalness free from error,
Definiteness toward complete enlightenment,

And the five clairvoyances
Throughout their continuum of lives.
May I ever in all ways bring
Help and happiness to all sentient beings.

May I always without harm
Simultaneously stop
All beings in all worlds
Who wish to commit sins.

May I always be an object of enjoyment
For all sentient beings according to their wish
And without interference as are the earth,
Water, fire, wind, medicine and forests.

May I be as dear to sentient beings as their
Own life and may they be very dear to me,
May their sins fructify for me
And all my virtues for them.

As long as any sentient being
Anywhere has not been liberated,
May I remain [in the world] for his sake
Even though I have attained enlightenment.

If the merit of this prayer
Had form, it would never fit
Into worlds as numerous
As sand grains in the Ganges.[78]

Nāgārjuna recommends the recitation of these twenty verses, as a devotional practice, three times a day, that is, morning, noon, and night. This pattern of practice comes from the Brahminic tradition, a tradition going back to the Vedic period, of reciting the mantra of salutation to the sun at sunrise, at midday, and at sunset. It should be said that all the verses of the text of the *Ratnamālā* would originally have been chanted, and in this way one learned them by heart.

The mantra is in a way a short and simple prayer, in which you identify yourself with the Buddha or Bodhisattva that you aspire to become.

It seems that the people of ancient India did not read silently, and when they read verses aloud, they chanted. In India today children still learn their lessons by repeating them aloud in a sort of sing-song.

These verses evidently provided Śāntideva with the model for the confession in the second chapter of his *Bodhicaryāvatāra*, from which the verses of the well-known Sevenfold Pūjā have been taken. The sequence varies slightly, as it does in other sources. Śāntideva's ordering runs thus: worship, salutation, going for refuge, confession of faults, rejoicing in merits, entreaty and supplication, and finally transference of merits. Nāgārjuna's, on the other hand, starts with going for refuge, then worship and salutation. Nor do Nāgārjuna's verses cover the different sections of the Sevenfold Pūjā equally. Some of them are referred to merely in passing, most of his verses being taken up with the transference of merits. But in passages like these it becomes clear that Śāntideva and Nāgārjuna belong to the same tradition. Both combine penetrating philosophical insight with intense devotion.

I am not sure that I would recommend reciting the Sevenfold Pūjā three times daily on a regular basis. The danger would be that it would become a chore. What I would say is that if you really felt like performing a pūjā, it would not matter so much if you did not get round to doing it, but if you did *not* feel in the mood, you probably ought to find time for it. As in the case of meditation, resistance is best confronted.

One should not forget that in the *Ratnamālā* Nāgārjuna is offering the king teachings that will be suitable for him in the event of his deciding to become a monk. If he was reciting the Sevenfold Pūjā on his own he would presumably have to set up the shrine himself. And when you have to set things up yourself, you will naturally tend to enter into the appropriate devotional mood.

Nāgārjuna's emphasis is heavily on the conclusion of the sequence. For him the transference or dedication of merit is very much the point of the whole practice, and it becomes what the Tibetans call a prayer of good wishes, expressing a supremely positive attitude towards all living beings. For Nāgārjuna, becoming Enlightened is the way in which one can help beings most effectively. On his becoming a Buddha he wants his very name to bring joy to beings. Such is the power of a word, a name; and hence the power of a mantra. A mantra is in a sense the name of the Buddha or Bodhisattva, and when you recite or repeat it, it puts you in touch with all the qualities of that Buddha or Bodhisattva. This is one of the reasons why the repetition of a mantra is considered to be so important. It is the essence of who they are. If you repeat the mantra, the Buddha or Bodhisattva will be there. The mantra is in a way a short and simple prayer, in which you identify yourself with the Buddha or Bodhisattva that you aspire to become.

Notes and references

References to *The Precious Garland* are verse numbers in Nāgārjuna's *The Precious Garland*, translated by Jeffrey Hopkins and Lati Rimpoche, with Anne Klein, Harper & Row, New York 1975.

1 *The Precious Garland*, verse 25.
2 This story is to be found in the Pāli canon, in the Great Chapter (*Mahāvagga*) of the *Vinaya Piṭaka* and also in the *Āyācana Sutta*, *Saṃyutta Nikāya*. A Mahāyāna source gives 'But how could liberation, which is so exquisite and profound, be expressed in words? It may be better not to give out my thoughts [he said to himself], and so he remained silent and at peace.' (Aśvaghoṣa, *Buddhacarita*, translated in William Theodore de Bary, *The Buddhist Tradition in India, China and Japan*, New York 1972, p.70.)
3 In many Buddhist traditions the nāgas are water deities who guard Buddhist scriptures that have been placed in their care until human beings are ready to receive them.
4 Asaṅga was born in the fourth century CE, in a Brahmin family from Peshawar. He began his Buddhist career as a Sarvāstivādin but 'departed from Nāgārjuna's view of absence of substantiality and advanced an idealistic doctrine' (from the entry in the *Rider Encyclopedia of Eastern Philosophy and Religion*).
5 *The Precious Garland*, verse 1.
6 *Nicomachean Ethics* Book 8.
7 Mahāvīra, the founder of Jainism, was the 24th and last Jaina Tīrthaṅkara ('Maker of the River Crossing') and a contemporary of the Buddha.

8 'East and West' is to be found in 'Lectures on Zen Buddhism', in *Zen Buddhism and Psychoanalysis*, by Erich Fromm, D.T. Suzuki and Richard de Martino, Harper & Row 1960, pp.1–5.

9 Tennyson, 'Flower in the Crannied Wall', 1869.

10 *The Precious Garland*, verse 5.

11 The Five Spiritual Faculties (*pañca-indriya*) are faith (Sanskrit *śraddhā*, Pāli *saddhā*), vigour (Sanskrit *vīrya*, Pāli *viriya*), mindfulness (Sanskrit smṛti, Pāli *sati*), concentration (*samādhi*), and wisdom (Sanskrit *prajñā*, Pāli *paññā*).

12 *The Precious Garland*, verse 6.

13 The four *brahma-vihāras* or 'sublime abodes' are four meditation practices through which one cultivates four positive emotions: loving kindness (*mettā*), compassion (*karuṇā*), sympathetic joy (*muditā*) and equanimity (*upekkhā*).

14 John Middleton Murry, *Things to Come: Essays*, Newman and Sidgwick, Ayer Publishing, 1928, p.34.

15 This is in the first chapter of the *Śūraṅgama Sūtra*: 'The Buddha said to Ānanda: "You and I are close relatives. Tell me what you saw in the assembly when you made up your mind to give up all worldly feelings of affection and love (to follow me)?" Ānanda replied: "I saw the thirty-two excellent characteristics and the shining crystal-like form of the Buddha's body. I thought that all this could not be the result of desire and love, for desire creates foul and fetid impurities like pus and blood which mingle and cannot produce the wondrous brightness of His golden-hued body, in admiration of which I shaved my head to follow Him."' (trans. Charles Luk)

16 'The *Mahāvastu Avadāna* ... describes itself as a work of the *Vinaya Piṭaka* of the Lokottaravādins, a branch of the Mahāsāṃghikas ... The *Mahāvastu* is probably the sole significant example of a primitive biography that has been made to incorporate ... legends in the form of Jātakas and Avadānas.' (Sangharakshita, *The Eternal Legacy*, Tharpa, London 1985, p.64.)

17 This is the story of the encounter between Milarepa and Dharma Wonshu (later Repa Shiwa Aui or the Cotton Clad Light of Peace); see Garma C.C. Chang, *The Hundred Thousand Songs of Milarepa*, Vol. 1, Shambhala 1999, p.179.

18 *The Precious Garland*, verse 26.

19 Nāropa (1016–1100), the *mahāsiddha* and transmitter of Mahāmudrā teachings, was the teacher of Marpa who was in turn the teacher of Milarepa. His dream yoga 'can lead one to purify the habitual thoughts of Saṃsāra, to realize that all things are manifestations of the mind, and that mind is devoid of self-entity like dreams ...' (Garma C.C. Chang, *The Six Yogas of Nāropa*, New York, 1977, p.94.)

20 *The Precious Garland*, verse 27.

21 This story is told in the *Meghiya Sutta* of the Pāli canon (*Udāna* 4:1). The Buddha's disciple Meghiya wants to go and meditate in a mango grove which seems to him especially suitable for meditation. The Buddha asks him to wait a while 'until some other bhikkhu comes', but Meghiya is insistent, and the Buddha eventually says, 'Do what you think it is time for'. Meghiya duly goes to meditate in the 'pleasing and charming' mango grove, but to his dismay is unable to concentrate. On his return, he tells the Buddha what happened, and the Buddha advises him that 'when the heart's release is immature, five things conduce to its maturity' – the five things being spiritual friendship, ethics, steadfastness, Dharma-talk, and awareness of the arising and passing away of things.

22 The *mettā bhāvanā* is a traditional Buddhist meditation practice which involves the cultivation of feelings of *mettā* or loving kindness towards all living beings.

23 *The Precious Garland*, verse 28.

24 *The Precious Garland*, verse 29.

25 Stream-entry (Sanskrit *srotāpanna*, Pāli *sotāpanna*). 'The Stream-entrant has developed insight sufficiently powerful to break, completely and finally, the three fetters of wrong belief concerning the nature of individuality (Sanskrit *satkāya-dṛṣṭi*, Pāli *sakkāya-diṭṭhi*), sceptical doubt (Sanskrit *vicikitsā*, Pāli *vicikicchā*) in the sense of wilfully incomplete, or hesitant, acceptance of the Doctrine, and dependence upon mere morality and external ascetic observances (Sanskrit *śīlavrata-parāmarśa*, Pāli *sīlabbata-parāmāsa*) as though they were by themselves a sufficient means to Enlightenment. Such a disciple is exempt from rebirth in any of the lower worlds, and has not more than seven lives to pass through, all on the human and divine planes, before attaining the total emancipation of mind which is Nirvāṇa. His characteristics are unshakeable faith in the Buddha, the Dharma and the Sangha, and an absolutely unblemished morality.' (Sangharakshita, *A Survey of Buddhism*, Windhorse, Birmingham 2001, p. 204.)

26 *The Precious Garland*, verses 31–3.

27 Ānanda was one of the most important disciples of the historical Buddha. He was the Buddha's cousin and entered the Buddhist order two years after its founding. Ānanda became the Buddha's personal attendant, and was famous for his extraordinary memory, by virtue of which he was able to retain the Buddha's discourses and thus began the oral tradition by means of which the Buddha's teachings were preserved for the first few centuries. He is said to have attained arhatship only after the death of the Buddha.

28 'The expression used everywhere in Buddhist texts referring to persons who realized Truth is "The dustless and stainless Eye

of Truth (*dhamma-cakkhu*) has arisen."' (Walpola Rahula, *What the Buddha Taught*, London 1967, p.9.)

29 *The Precious Garland*, verse 34.

30 ibid., verse 35.

31 ibid., verse 36.

32 ibid., verse 37.

33 ibid., verse 38.

34 'Only four views regarding the relation between cause and effect are possible [according to Nāgārjuna in the *Kārikās*]: that cause and effect are identical; that they are different; that they are both identical and different; and that they are neither identical nor different. The first view ... was held at the time of Nāgārjuna by the Sāṃkhya School; some centuries later Śaṃkara incorporated it into his non-dualist Vedanta.' (Sangharakshita, *A Survey of Buddhism*, Windhorse, Birmingham 2001, p. 351.)

35 *The Precious Garland*, verses 39–40.

36 ibid., verses 41–2.

37 'A party of travellers is bound for a place called Ratnadvīpa ('The Place of Jewels'), and has employed a guide to show them the way through the dense forest. It is a very difficult, dangerous road, and long before they have reached their destination the travellers become exhausted, and say to their guide 'We can't go on another step. Let's all go back.' But the guide thinks 'That would be a pity. They've come so far already. What can I do to persuade them to keep going?' Well, apparently the guide has some sort of magic power, because what he does is conjure up a magic city. He says to the travellers 'Look! There's a city right here in front of us. Let's rest there and have something to eat, and then we'll decide what to do next.' The travellers, of course, are only too pleased to stop and have a rest. They have a meal and spend the night in the magic city, and in the morning they feel much better, and decide that they will carry on with their journey after all. So the guide makes the magic city disappear and leads the travellers to their destination, the Place of Jewels.

The meaning of the parable is not hard to fathom in the context of the sutra. The guide is of course the Buddha, the travellers are the disciples. The Place of Jewels is Supreme Enlightenment and the magic city is the Hīnayāna nirvāṇa – nirvāṇa as the comparatively negative state of freedom from passions, without positive spiritual illumination. And, as the parable suggests, the Buddha first of all speaks of nirvāṇa in the ordinary psychological sense. Only when this teaching has been assimilated – only when his disciples have rested in the magic city – does he lead them on to the higher spiritual goal of perfect Buddhahood, the Place of Jewels.' (Sangharakshita, *The*

Drama of Cosmic Enlightenment: Parables, Myths and Symbols of the White Lotus Sutra, Glasgow 1993, pp.44–5).

38 'As interpreted by the gifted early Buddhist nun Dhammadinnā, whose views were fully endorsed by the Buddha with the remark that he had nothing further to add to them, the doctrine of conditioned co-production represents an all-inclusive reality that admits of two different trends in the whole of existence ... The Saṃsāra or 'Round of Conditioned Existence' represents the first trend. Herein, as depicted by the 'Wheel of Life', sentient beings under the influence of craving, hatred, and bewilderment revolve as gods, men, *asuras*, animals, *pretas*, and denizens of hell in accordance with the law of karma and experience pleasure and pain ... The path to deliverance and Nirvāṇa together represent the second trend, Nirvāṇa being not only a counter-process of cessation of the cyclic order of existence ... but the farthest discernible point of the progressive one.' (Sangharakshita, *A Survey of Buddhism*, Windhorse, Birmingham 2001, pp.12–3).

The twelve positive *nidānas* are: 'Dependent upon *duḥkha* [suffering] arises *śraddhā* (Pāli *saddhā*) or faith ... Then dependent upon faith arises *prāmodya* (Pāli *pāmojja*) or joy; dependent on joy arises *prīti* (Pāli *pīti*) or rapture; dependent upon rapture arises serenity; dependentupon serenity arises happiness; dependent upon happiness arises concentration; dependent upon concentration arises knowledge and vision of things as they really are; dependent upon knowledge and vision of things as they really are arises repulsion; dependent upon repulsion arises *vairāgya* (Pāli *virāga*) or passionlessness); dependent upon passionlessness arises liberation; and dependent upon liberation arises knowledge of the destruction of the *āśravas* (Pāli *āsavas*): the intoxicants of sensuous craving, thirst for existence, and ignorance.' (Sangharakshita, *A Survey of Buddhism*, Windhorse, Birmingham 2001, p.139.) For a detailed account, see also Sangharakshita, *What is the Dharma?*, Windhorse, Birmingham 1998, chapter 7.

39 *The Precious Garland*, verses 52–4.

40 ibid., verse 55.

41 ibid., verses 58-60.

42 ibid., verse 61.

43 Lokāyata, literally 'belonging to the world of sense', is the name given to a materialistic system said to have been founded by Cārvāka.

44 'Owl-Followers' refers to Vaiśeṣikas, a non-Buddhist school founded by Kaṇāda (meaning 'atom eater') in around the 2nd century CE. His cosmological system, set out in the *Vaiśeṣika Sūtra*, is one of the six classic systems of philosophy making up the orthodox tradition of Indian thought.

45 See note 7.

46 *The Precious Garland*, verse 62.

47 ibid., verses 63–5.

48 'As a washerman uses dirt / To wash clean a garment, / So, with impurity, / The wise man makes himself pure.' (From a late seventh century Indian Tantric text *Disquisition on the Purification of the Intellect (Cittaviśuddhiprakaraṇa)* by Āryadeva, translated in William Theodore de Bary, *The Buddhist Tradition in India*, China and Japan, New York, 1972, p.120.)

49 *The Precious Garland*, verses 66–70.

50 ibid., verse 61.

51 The Abhidharma is the third of the three baskets (Tripiṭaka) or collections of the Buddha's words. Abhidharma means 'about Dharma', though traditionally the term was often interpreted as 'higher Dharma' in the sense of a philosophically more exact exposition of the teaching. The Abhidharma Piṭaka is 'a collection of highly scholastic treatises which annotate and explain the *Āgama/Nikāya* texts, define technical terms, arrange numerically classified doctrines in numerical order, give a systematic philosophical exposition of the teaching and establish a consistent method of spiritual practice. Above all, they interpret the Dharma in terms of strict pluralistic realism and work out an elaborate philosophy of relations.' (Sangharakshita, *A Survey of Buddhism*, Birmingham 2001, pp. 20–1.)

52 *The Precious Garland*, verses 72–3.

53 ibid., verses 74–5.

54 ibid., verse 76.

55 ibid., verses 78–9.

56 ibid., verses 80–92.

57 Śāntideva (approx. 685–763 CE) 'is well known as the author of the *Śikṣā-Samuccaya* and the *Bodhicaryāvatāra*, two of the most popular works in the whole range of Mahāyāna literature. Śāntideva ... knows both the heights and the depths of spiritual experience.' (Sangharakshita, *A Survey of Buddhism*, Windhorse, Birmingham 2001, pp.358–9.) The arguments against anger occur in chapter 6 of the *Bodhicaryāvatāra*:

> Both the weapon and my body
> Are causes of my suffering.
> Since he gave rise to the weapon and I to the body,
> With whom should I be angry?

Śāntideva, (translated by Stephen Batchelor), *A Guide to the Bodhisattva's Way of Life*, New Delhi, 1979, p.68.

58 Walt Whitman, 'On the Terrible Doubt of Appearances', in Book V, 'Calamus', of *Leaves of Grass*.

59 *The Precious Garland*, verses 93–5.

60 ibid., verses 96–7.

61 ibid., verses 98–100.

62 ibid., verses 101–3.

63 ibid., verses 104-6.

64 Such questions are known as the 'inexpressibles' or undetermined (Pāli *avyākata*, Sanskrit *avyākṛta*) questions. (The *Poṭṭhapāda Sutta*, the 9th *sutta* of the *Dīgha Nikāya* lists them and so does the *Cūḷa-Maluṅkya Sutta*, the 63rd *sutta* of the *Majjhima Nikāya*.)

65 *The Precious Garland*, verses 107–15.

66 ibid., verses 116–22.

67 For the appearance of Brahmā Sahampati, see *Āyācana Sutta, Saṃyutta-Nikāya* 6.1; and for the difficulty of grasping the truth of conditionality, see also the *Mahānidāna Sutta*, the 15th *sutta* of the *Dīgha Nikāya*: [Ānanda:] How deep is this causal law, and how deep it seems! And yet do I regard it as quite plain to understand! [The Buddha:] Say not so, Ānanda! Say not so! Deep indeed is this causal law, and deep it appears to be. It is by not knowing, by not understanding, by not penetrating this doctrine, that this world of men has become entangled like a ball of twine, become covered with mildew, become like munja grass and rushes, and unable to pass beyond the doom of the Waste, the Way of Woe, the Fall, and the Ceaseless Round (of rebirth).

68 Śūnyavāda literally means the way (*vāda*) of emptiness (*śūnya*). 'This conditionality or unreality of all phenomena the Mahāyānists indicate by the term *śūnyatā* or Emptiness. Doctrines such as the Four Truths and conditioned co-production, since they refer to unrealities, are themselves unreal in the ultimate sense, and whatever truth they possess is not absolute but only conventional. *Śūnyatā* or *tathatā* alone is the Absolute Truth.' (Sangharakshita, *A Survey of Buddhism*, Windhorse, Birmingham 2001, p. 298.)

69 *The Precious Garland*, verses 123–4.

70 ibid., verses 346–52.

71 ibid., verse 353.

72 ibid., verses 354–5.

73 See Sangharakshita, *Know Your Mind* (Windhorse, Birmingham 1998) for more information.

74 John Stuart Mill, *Examination of Sir William Hamilton's Philosophy*, Vol. I. Chap. XI.

75 *The Precious Garland*, verse 356.

76 ibid., verses 357–63.

77 ibid., verses 364–6.

78 ibid., verses 465–86.

Index

WINDHORSE PUBLICATIONS

Windhorse Publications is a Buddhist charitable company based in the UK. We place great emphasis on producing books of high quality that are accessible and relevant to those interested in Buddhism at whatever level. We are the main publisher of the works of Sangharakshita, the founder of the Triratna Buddhist Order and Community. Our books draw on the whole range of the Buddhist tradition, including translations of traditional texts, commentaries, books that make links with contemporary culture and ways of life, biographies of Buddhists, and works on meditation.

As a not-for-profit enterprise, we ensure that all surplus income is invested in new books and improved production methods, to better communicate Buddhism in the 21st Century. We welcome donations to help us continue our work – to find out more, go to www.windhorsepublications.com.

The Windhorse is a mythical animal that flies over the earth carrying on its back three precious jewels, bringing these invaluable gifts to all humanity: the Buddha (the 'awakened one') his teaching, and the community of all his followers.

Windhorse Publications
169 Mill Road
Cambridge CB1 3AN
UK
info@windhorsepublications.com

Perseus Distribution
210 American Drive
Jackson TN 38301
USA

Windhorse Books
PO Box 574
Newtown NSW 2042
Australia

Also from Windhorse Publications

Living with Awareness
A Guide to the Satipatthana Sutta

by Sangharakshita

Paying attention to how things look, sound, and feel makes them more enjoyable; it is as simple (and as difficult) as that. Mindfulness and the breath – this deceptively simple yet profound teaching in the Satipatthana Sutta is the basis of much insight meditation practice today. By looking at aspects of our daily life, such as Remembering, Looking, Dying, and Reflecting, Sangharakshita shows how broad an application the practice of mindfulness can have – and how our experience can be enriched by its presence.

ISBN 9781 899579 38 9
£11.99 / $18.95 / €17.95
200 pages

Living with Kindness
The Buddha's teaching on Metta

by Sangharakshita

Kindness is one of the most basic qualities we can possess and one of the most powerful. In Buddhism it is called *metta* – an opening of the heart to all that we meet. In this commentary on the *Karaniya Metta Sutta*, Sangharakshita shows how nurturing kindness can help develop a more fulfilled and compassionate heart.

Will help both Buddhists and people of other faiths to come to a deeper understanding of the true significance of kidness as a way of life and a way of meditation. – Pure Land Notes

ISBN 9781 899579 64 8
£12.99 / $19.95 / €15.95
160 pages

Living Ethically
Advice from Nagarjuna's Precious Garland

by Sangharakshita

In a world of increasingly confused ethics, *Living Ethically* looks back over the centuries for guidance from Nagarjuna, one of the greatest teachers of the Mahayana tradition. Drawing on the themes of Nagarjuna's famous scripture, *Precious Garland of Advice for a King*, this book explores the relationship between an ethical lifestyle and the development of wisdom. Covering both personal and collective ethics, Sangharakshita considers such enduring themes as pride, power and business, as well as friendship, love and generosity.

Sangharakshita is the founder of the Triratna Buddhist Community, a worldwide Buddhist movement. He has a lifetime of teaching experience and is the author of over 40 books.

ISBN 9781 899579 86 0
£12.99 / $20.95 / €15.95
216 pages

A Guide to the Buddhist Path

by Sangharakshita

The Buddhist tradition, with its numerous schools and teachings, can understandably feel daunting. Which teachings really matter? How can one begin to practise Buddhism in a systematic way? This can be confusing territory. Without a guide one can easily get dispirited or lost.

Profoundly experienced in Buddhist practice, intimately familiar with its main schools, and founder of the Triratna Buddhist Community, Sangharakshita is the ideal guide. In this highly readable anthology he sorts out fact from myth and theory from practice to reveal the principle ideals and teachings of Buddhism. The result is a reliable and far-reaching guide to this inspiring path.

ISBN 9781 907314 05 6
£16.99 / $23.95 / €19.95
264 pages

Buddhist Meditation
Tranquillity, Imagination & Insight

by Kamalashila

First published in 1991, this book is a comprehensive and practical guide to Buddhist meditation, providing a complete introduction for beginners, as well as detailed advice for experienced meditators seeking to deepen their practice. Kamalashila explores the primary aims of Buddhist meditation: enhanced awareness, true happiness, and – ultimately – liberating insight into the nature of reality. This third edition includes new sections on the importance of the imagination, on Just Sitting, and on reflection on the Buddha. Kamalashila has been teaching meditation since becoming a member of the Triratna Buddhist Order in 1974. He has developed approaches to meditation practice that are accessible to people in the contemporary world, whilst being firmly grounded in the Buddhist tradition.

A wonderfully practical and accessible introduction to the important forms of Buddhist meditation. From his years of meditation practice, Kamalashila has written a book useful for both beginners and longtime practitioners.
– Gil Fronsdal, author of *A Monastery Within*, founder of the Insight Meditation Center, California, USA.

ISBN 9781 907314 09 4
£17.99 / $27.95 / €19.95
272 pages

Buddhist Wisdom in Practice series

The Art of Reflection

by Ratnaguna

It is all too easy either to think obsessively, or to not think enough. But how do we think usefully? How do we reflect? Like any art, reflection can be learnt and developed, leading to a deeper understanding of life and to the fullness of wisdom. *The Art of Reflection* is a practical guide to reflection as a spiritual practice, about 'what we think and how we think about it'. It is a book about contemplation and insight, and reflection as a way to discover the truth.

No-one who takes seriously the study and practice of the Dharma should fail to read this ground-breaking book. – Sangharakshita, founder of the Triratna Buddhist Community

ISBN 9781 899579 89 1
£9.99 / $16.95 / €11.95
160 pages

This Being, That Becomes

by Dhivan Thomas Jones

Dhivan Thomas Jones takes us into the heart of the Buddha's insight that everything arises in dependence on conditions. With the aid of lucid reflections and exercises he prompts us to explore how conditionality works in our own lives, and provides a sure guide to the most essential teaching of Buddhism.

Clearly and intelligently written, this book carries a lot of good advice. – Prof Richard Gombrich, author of *What the Buddha Thought*

ISBN 9781 899579 90 7
£12.99 / $20.95 / €15.95
216 pages

Exploring Karma & Rebirth

by Nagapriya

Exploring Karma & Rebirth helps us to unravel the complexities of these two important but often misunderstood Buddhist doctrines. Clarifying, examining, and considering them, it offers an imaginative reading of what the teachings could mean for us now. Informative and thought provoking, *Exploring Karma & Rebirth* insists that, above all, to be of enduring value these doctrines must continue to serve the overriding aim of Buddhism: spiritual awakening.

Every Buddhist should read it. – David Loy

An excellent introduction. – Stephen Batchelor

Cogent, knowledgeable, and penetrating. – Norman Fischer

ISBN 9781 899579 61 7
£8.99 / $13.95 / €13.95
176 pages

Visions of Mahayana Buddhism

by Nagapriya

In a unique overview of this inspiring tradition, Nagapriya introduces its themes and huge spectrum of practices, literature and movements. Charting the evolution and expression of the Mahayana as a whole, he tracks its movement across South and East Asia, uncovering its history, culture and doctrines and blending this extensive knowledge with a strong element of lived practice. Ideal for both teaching and personal use, this far-reaching and imaginative guide provides a solid foundation for any study in Buddhism and a valuable voice on Asian history.

A very helpful introduction and overview of this complex, fascinating tradition. – David Loy, author of *Money, Sex, War, Karma*

ISBN 9781 899579 97 6
£12.99 / $21.95 / €16.95
288 pages

Satipaṭṭhāna
The Direct Path to Realization

by Anālayo

This best-selling book offers a unique and detailed textual study of the Satipaṭṭhāna Sutta, a foundational Buddhist discourse on meditation practice.

This book should prove to be of value both to scholars of Early Buddhism and to serious meditators alike. – Bhikku Bodhi

. . . a gem . . . I learned a lot from this wonderful book and highly recommend it. – Joseph Goldstein

An indispensible guide . . . surely destined to become the classic commentary on the Satipaṭṭhāna. – Christopher Titmuss

Very impressive and useful, with its blend of strong scholarship and attunement to practice issues. – Prof. Peter Harvey, author of *An Introduction to Buddhist Ethics*

ISBN 9781 899579 54 9
£17.99 / $27.95 / €19.95
336 pages

The Three Jewels series

by Sangharakshita

This set of three essential texts introduces the Three Jewels which are central to Buddhism: the *Buddha* (the Enlightened One), the *Dharma* (the Buddha's teachings), and the *Sangha* (the spiritual community).

Who is the Buddha?

ISBN 9781 899579 51 8
£8.99 / $14.95 / €11.95
188 pages

What is the Dharma?

ISBN 9781 899579 01 3
£9.99 / $19.95 / €12.95
272 pages

What is the Sangha?

ISBN 9781 899579 31 0
£9.99 / $19.95 / €12.95
288 pages

Meeting the Buddhas series

by Vessantara

This set of three informative guides, by one of our best-selling authors, introduces the historical and archetypal figures from within the Tibetan Buddhist tradition. Each book focuses on a different set of figures and features full-colour illustrations.

A Guide to the Buddhas

ISBN 9781 899579 83 9
£11.99 / $18.95 / 18.95
176 pages

A Guide to the Bodhisattvas

ISBN 9781 899579 84 6
£11.99 / $18.95 / 18.95
128 pages

A Guide to the Deities of the Tantra

ISBN 9781 899579 85 3
£11.99 / $18.95 / 18.95
192 pages